Not Intimidating

Not Intimidating

Teaching Different Reading Genres to a Diverse Student Body

Anna J. Small Roseboro

ROWMAN & LITTLEFIELD
Lanham • Boulder • New York • London

Published by Rowman & Littlefield
An imprint of The Rowman & Littlefield Publishing Group, Inc.
4501 Forbes Boulevard, Suite 200, Lanham, Maryland 20706
www.rowman.com

6 Tinworth Street, London SE11 5AL, United Kingdom

Copyright © 2019 by Anna J. Small Roseboro

All rights reserved. No part of this book may be reproduced in any form or by any electronic or mechanical means, including information storage and retrieval systems, without written permission from the publisher, except by a reviewer who may quote passages in a review.

British Library Cataloguing-in-Publication Information Available

Library of Congress Cataloging-in-Publication Data Available

ISBN: 978-1-4758-4282-1 (cloth : alk. paper)
ISBN: 978-1-4758-4283-8 (pbk. : alk. paper)
ISBN: 978-1-4758-4284-5 (electronic)

Contents

Foreword		vii
Acknowledgments		ix
Introduction		xi
1	Preparing the Roadbed for Smoother Travel	1
2	Unpacking the Story and Understanding the Genre	25
3	Crossing into Novel Territory: Reading Longer Fiction	45
4	Teaching Classical Fiction: Where the Ghosts of the Past Speak Today	75
5	Opening the Past Imaginatively: Teaching Historical Fiction	95
6	Taking T.I.M.E. to Teach Poetry	113
7	Playing It Right: Reading and Writing about Drama	137
8	Unreeling Nonfiction: Essays, Speeches, and the Media	155
Afterword		173
Bibliography		177
About the Author		183

Foreword

I remember my father giving me good advice when I was young, stubborn, struggling with a fly rod, and repeatedly getting the fly caught in the brush. He told me that when learning something new, I should look around me, pay attention to what is working for others, be willing to try some different techniques, and develop my own style. He said that I might just learn a trick or two from my observations and patience. I resisted for awhile and continued to struggle until I understood his advice about learning, advice that has been key to my ability to succeed not only at fly fishing but also at teaching. Educators frequently joke about the best teachers being the best thieves, but what is really true is that effective educators never stop learning from each other. They mentor, share best practices, and provide tools like *Not Intimidating: Teaching Different Reading Genres to a Diverse Student Body* by Anna J. Small Roseboro, a tool that would have been valuable for me in my first teaching journey.

I began my educational career at a university as a teaching assistant with no skills as a teacher—no training, no mentors, just my memories of favorite teachers in high school and college. I did not have any concrete pedagogical knowledge, and it was difficult to go to class each day, but as I struggled, I remembered my father's advice. I discovered some techniques that worked, watched other educators, and gained instructional support in books about teaching composition. When I began teaching high school, a veteran educator became a mentor who willingly shared her lessons and strategies with me, and we collaborated regularly. That collegial relationship made me understand how valuable it is to mentor and share.

It was during my tenure on the board of California Association of Teachers of English (CATE) that I met Anna Roseboro and discovered how much we had in common. We enjoyed talking about teaching, how to tackle difficult literature, how to use writing circles, or what to do when a student doesn't want to read or write. While we initially discussed our own classes, we eventually began to focus on our shared vision of doing a better job of mentoring early career educators, of helping them to be successful. Out of our mutual concerns, we took action. I began working with California's Teacher Induction program, and she began to write. Our conversations and her concerns to help early educators thrive grew into her writing about the skills and resources that new teachers need. From the management and engagement of students to teaching academic vocabulary to a diverse student population, *Not Intimidating* provides support and generates confidence.

The book details the how of teaching that we often discussed during our CATE meetings. It combines theory and classroom application, making it a tool for any teacher at any level because it focuses on how, not what to teach. When providing ideas for a specific novel or poem in the book, Anna Roseboro makes it clear that the example is just that—an example, not a blueprint for teaching a specific work. She gives ideas for tackling a skill using unique choices and adaptations. In the information about using literature circles, for example, she discusses techniques to model the roles in groups to make them more effective and how to use charts and colors to generate reading responses and deep thinking by students. In her explanation of rubrics, Roseboro not only shares ways to create and use them for both formative and summative assessment but also how to engage students in the process. The book is a treasure trove of ideas based on classroom expertise and research.

Not Intimidating is valuable in the hands of any English language arts teacher. Early career educators can sometimes feel lonely and overwhelmed, especially if they lack support to help them gain confidence, but the book has so much well-organized information that they will discover a mentor within the pages of the book. At the same time, mentors searching for resources for their beginning teachers and apprentice teachers will value the book for its usable content. Rich with information, classroom examples, and techniques that incorporate firsthand experience with strong educational standards, this is a book that English teachers need.

Joan Williams
Eureka, California
Veteran English Language Arts Teacher
Mentor in California Beginning Teacher Support
and Assessment (BTSA) Induction Program

Acknowledgments

Teaching is both a vocation and avocation, a gift from God that I must share. Wrapping this gift is a circle of staunch friends and colleagues. Among those critical to preparing this updated edition of my 2013 book on writing are Claudia A. Marschall, my sister-friend, Laury Isenberg, who has stood with me since we met in the San Diego Area Writing Project and later taught together at The Bishop's School, and Quentin Schultze, my colleague at Calvin College, who convinced and helped me to finish that first editions that have led to invitations to publish five more books for teachers!

Teachers of students in middle school through college representing diverse ethnicities in towns and cities across the nation consented to field test ideas described in this book. They sent their own reflections and students' comments, responses, and writing samples that confirm the cultural relevance of these lessons. I am especially pleased to have early career educators: Cresence Birder, José Luís Cano, Kiondre Dunham, Cassidy Earle, and Emily Espy share their insight for this book. In this circle also are mid-career and veteran teachers like Anne Brown, Audrey Spica, and Ellen Murray who inspire me with their generosity. I am grateful to you all.

I appreciate, too, the confidence of Tom Koerner and Carlie Wall, editors at Rowman & Littlefield, who expressed confidence in my work and invited me to write *Not Intimidating*.

Introduction

> He liked the mere act of reading,
> the magic of turning scratches on a page into words inside his head.
>
> —John Green[1]

Teaching students to read and understand different genres of literature need not be the intimidating experience it is for some new teachers. Whether you are preparing for student teaching, transitioning from teaching older or younger students, or a college graduate student teaching your first section of an introductory English course, you can find ideas to adopt or adapt. You see, it does not matter if you have studied the selections on your required list; if you understand how to lead explorations that reveal distinctive qualities of each genre, you can have productive learning experiences with your students. You can share the magic with them, inspiring a comparable response to reading different genres that John Green describes in my opening quotation.

Perhaps the most important thought to keep in mind is that the definition of genre is broad and generally describes writing that shares distinguishable characteristics. The two common divisions are fiction and nonfiction. Then there are the subcategories of prose, poetry, drama, and essay. But these four subcategories occur in both fiction and/or nonfiction. So the purpose of teaching students about literature categorized as genre is simply to share with them features or characteristics to ease their reading, comprehension, and appreciation of these texts. When students know what to expect, they are not as surprised by what unfolds.

Deciding ahead of time how you will (1) structure lessons, (2) pace class time, (3) assess learning, (4) evaluate your teaching, and (5) manage grades can ease the way for you and your students. Laying appropriate groundwork can make it less stressful navigating along the way. Here are ideas to help you scope out the year as you consider the genres you are to teach and prepare the road bed for safe and satisfying travel over the course of the school year.

Not Intimidating: Teaching Different Reading Genres to a Diverse Student Body (*NI*) describes ways to

- establish a nurturing classroom environment for diverse students, reflected in race, religion, gender, language, and culture;
- develop firm but fair grading guidelines that keep students, parents, and administrators apprised of both grades and growth;
- plan reading lessons that include strategies to adopt or adapt to your own classes in ways that keep you interested in the various genres you may be required to teach; and
- balance student choice within teacher control in terms of texts, assessments, and class activities.

Here are

- samples of formative and summative assessments measuring student growth in reading comprehension;
- ways to select relevant texts that serve as an inspiration for living and patterns for writing; and
- lessons designed to engage students from various cultural, ethnic, regional, and economic populations.

Most important, here are ideas to help you manage the load by sharing the burden.

As a National Board Certified Teacher vetted by the National Board for Professional Teaching Standards, a National Writing Project Fellow, ten years as codirector and mentor of the National Council of Teachers of English Early Career Educators Leadership Award program, and a Literacy Center of West Michigan–trained adult English Language Learners tutor, I remain current regarding the issues facing educators teaching students born in the twenty-first century. I bring to this writing an amalgamation of my teaching and learning experiences.

Personal experiences guide my writing. I have taught in five states—California, Massachusetts, Michigan, Missouri, and New York—in urban, suburban, public, private, and parochial schools, middle school through college graduate classes. I have mentored early career educators across the nation. Sixteen years as director of Summer Sessions for students grades five to twelve and five years as an English department chair instill a broad view of how knowledge and skill in teaching writing for different purposes and across content areas benefits writing teachers no matter the ages of their students. I have observed the challenges of teachers committed to their students' success. This book reflects what I learned in these roles.

I am an active member in local, state, and national professional organizations for educators, as well as have served in a variety of elected and appointed positions, including president of the California Association of Teachers of English and several roles in the Conference on English Leadership. Participants in interactive workshops I presented, based on the lessons described in this book, let me know there is hunger for this knowledge and experience.

College professors find *NI* ideas useful for preparing and supporting educators who teach middle school, high school, or community college students. These teachers benefit as they explore ideas related to selecting texts and planning engaging lessons while managing grades, varying class activities, and using time efficiently with students new to the challenges in more demanding academic settings.

The progression of lessons in *NI* reflects the philosophy of gradual release of responsibility. In this pedagogical approach, the teacher models spiraling steps in the learning process. Thoughtful teachers plan in-class small group and independent practice *before* assuming students can work independently on reading tasks that assure the teacher that they can meet standards and learning goals for the course.

Equally important, *NI* describes ways teachers can include art and writing to learn and reflect on learning. From this philosophical stance, all writing does *not* have to be read and/or graded by the teacher, and art is a powerful way to teach and let students show what they know. Here you will see effective and efficient ways to manage class time and assess student learning as they read for different purposes, and write to capture their own stories in different genres by patterning what they learn from published writers they study with you and read on their own.

Several published texts address issues teaching reading genres in middle school, or within pre-service content area literacy methods classes. But few—all in one book—address incorporating a map managing the load, facilitating understanding different genres and subcategories, or narrating guided steps for class management. grading, suggesting model and alternative texts, and sample student responses.

While most teacher education programs across the nation offer credentialing programs structured to prepare to teach in elementary schools or high schools, few have course work designed specifically to prepare for teaching students in the middle school, freshmen in high school, or introductory community colleges classes. This book and the companion website www.teachingenglishlanguagearts.com can help fill those gaps.

I invite you to consider the concepts here that can guide and, coach, support, and sustain you along this professional career path, and enable you to become and remain an engaged, enthusiastic, and effective teacher of students in the middle school and beyond. Explore strategies to develop and present lessons that meet students' emotional and intellectual needs while challenging them to complete increasingly complex tasks in a more culturally responsive classroom setting,

When students are learning, and you can document that learning through appropriate assessments, both you and your students enjoy more of your time together on the journey of a school year. Here in *NI* you may discover designs and expand your instruction options with pragmatic and proven practices that bring you the kind of pleasure in teaching and mentoring early career educators that I have experienced for more than four decades.

NOTE

1. John Green, *A Place for Us*. https://www.goodreads.com/quotes/tag/literature (accessed June 18, 2018).

Chapter 1

Preparing the Roadbed for Smoother Travel

You often hear the expression that books can serve as windows and/or mirrors. This is true, but quagmires can bog down inexperienced teachers who think this concept is an either/or situation. Some think if the text is by someone of the same race, religion, or region as the readers, the text will be a mirror; if the author is different from the student, the reading experience will be a view through a window. But that seldom is the case, because a single author does not speak for or to every one of his or her ethnic or social group.

A distinctive experience opened my eyes when I assumed that a writing by an African American, Toni Morrison, would be a wide-open window experience for Anglo-American students in my class.

A PERSONAL STORY

For a culminating assignment one year, my students got to choose an author who had won a prestigious writing award during the students' lifetime. One Caucasian student selected Toni Morrison and chose to read The Bluest Eye.

On the day of her oral presentation, the student held up the requisite visual aid. In her case, it was a poster depicting large bright blue eyes with dilated pupils in which she had drawn a picture of herself. From one eye dripped a faint trail of tears.

You may know that Pecola, the main character in the Morrison novel, is a young African American girl with low self-esteem, the victim of verbal and physical bullying who believes she is ugly. She thinks she can be beautiful only if she were to have blue eyes. She tries various strategies to change her physical appearance to better fit that norm of beauty, and, in doing so, becomes mentally deranged.

My Euro-American student saw herself in African American Pecola. This teenager had accepted a social norm that being thin is a sign of physical beauty and she nearly killed herself by not eating. Subsequent emotional and physical distress led to hospitalization for anorexia. Thankfully, medical attention and counseling helped her overcome those feeling of self-hate. Reading during her recovery, the young lady related in her report that she identified with Pecola's pain. But unlike the fictional character, my student returned to emotional and physical health and to our class where she shared her story. Before she finished her report, most of us listening became as teary as her visual depiction of weeping blue eyes.

This student's presentation demonstrated to me that books can serve as a mirror in the least expected ways. We educators cannot preclude the power of a text for our students. In other words, any book may be a window and/or a mirror to any student. So, when you have the option to select texts, choose them because they are well written; let the authors speak for themselves and allow students to choose, write, and talk about what the texts say or reveal to them.

This experience confirmed for me the quotation from Dr. Rudine Sims Bishop who wrote, "When lighting conditions are just right, however, a window can also be a mirror. Literature transforms human experience and reflects it back to us, and in that reflection we can see our own lives and experiences as part of a larger human experience."[1] You can be the light for your students; they can also be the light for you.

The challenge, of course, will be designing lessons that help students understand how authors use words, sentence structure, and order to tell their stories and make their cases. That is the reason teaching the language of literature will help students understand the devices used and acquire a vocabulary to discuss literature.

In the lessons to come will be ways to teach your students as you review and model, then give students opportunities to practice using these terms in conversation and writing, and then as tools for drafting their own stories. To be able to read is a good thing; to comprehend what one reads is better; to explore how stories work just expands that enlightening experience of reading.

SET THE GROUNDWORK
FOR OPEN CONVERSATIONS

To make this a positive instructional year for you, consider ways you can incorporate *writing to learn* into your course. This is writing in which students explain, explore, and expand their thinking about the texts you assign, but you only need to read what they write, not grade it for correctness. This *writing to learn* serves multiple purposes in an English course.

The first is helping students prepare to talk with their peers and in class discussion. The strategy may be one you know already—Think, Pair, Share or Turn and Talk. Just allow a few moments for students to write before they are expected to verbalize their thinking. This teaching strategy is particularly useful in classes with shy, new-to-the-school English language learners.

Writing to Explore, Explain, and Expand Reading

Many such students can read and understand quite well when they have dictionaries nearby and access to the Internet when they read. But being asked to verbalize their thinking without having time to access the words in English, arrange them in their minds, and figure out how to pronounce the words correctly evokes near trauma for some students. On the other hand, if you allot a couple minutes for all students to write a few words, phrases, or sentences, those who need a little more time to organize their thinking will be prepared to share their insights with more confidence.

Understanding Students of Different Ages

If you teach students in different grades, you have seen the range of understanding in students across the grade levels. The younger students are likely to be more literal at the beginning of the year than are the older students, and therefore these younger students will need to be taught differently.

Students in grade nine usually are only thirteen or fourteen years old, and many have not yet developed the cerebral lobes to process abstract concepts. They may benefit from sentences that start like these: "This makes me think of . . ."; "it surprised me when . . ."; "I wonder why . . ."; and so on. Your English language learners appreciate this kind of linguistic support, too. Modeling this kind of talking about texts for all students reminds those who know it and teaches those who do not.

Your older students will be able to recognize and discuss themes on a more abstract level, once they are reminded of what they're looking for. Consider posting or projecting such prompts as:

- In this piece of literature, what is it about the conflict and response to it that would be true, regardless of time or place? (Universality.)
- What incidents in the beginning, middle, and end of this piece suggest that yours is a valid theme statement? (To validate their observation, you could ask for quotations, direct references, and page numbers.)
- What role(s) do(es) certain character(s) play in revealing that theme? (Recognizing the role's of major and minor characters.)

- Where have you seen similar behavior in literature and in life? (Validating observation-making connections to what they have read, seen, or experienced.)

Younger, less-experienced readers probably will be fine with SWBST strategy. They may recall from elementary school describing the events in a story with *Somebody Wanted, But, So, Then*. Ask them if they remember or teach it to them. Modulate to the more sophisticated structures as students mature.

Go ahead and accept any theme statement that can be validated, even if it seems far-fetched on first hearing it. Accepted new, but verifiable theme statements encourage students to think for themselves, knowing they will be required to support their opinions with direct references from the texts.

Enjoy this time with your students as you implement activities that help these learners probe more deeply and understand more fully the beauty of writing and the joy of reading.

Adapt LIT CIRCLE

LIT CIRCLE, a discussion strategy attributed to Harvey "Smokey" Daniels, is an effective way to get students interacting with texts from different perspectives. He describes five basic roles: Summarizer, Illustrator, Travel Tracer, Word Wizard, and Connector. Once modeled, this LIT CIRCLE strategy works well with students of all ages from a variety of cultures and ease with language! See figure 1.1 for a way to structure a unit so all readers have an opportunity to experience each of the roles once they see you demonstrate them.

Consider modeling one role each day during the first week students are reading their books during class. Yes, starting books together tends to get students off to a more solid start. You could post a couple of guiding questions on the board to remind students to pay attention to elements of exposition they will find in the opening chapter(s) of their novels. Then allow twenty minutes for them to read. However, once you complete the exposition, encourage them to read at their own pace.

Next, model ROLE #1 and have small groups or those reading the same text meet and talk about the book from that perspective. Close the class session with a guiding question that invites them to connect what they read to something they have observed or experienced. Begin the next class period with a journal prompt asking them to write about that connection.

Class Meetings 2–4

- Reflect on last reading.
- Read for twenty minutes.
- Model the next LIT CIRCLE role

- Have students meet in groups to discuss reading the assigned text from the perspective just modeled.
- Close with a prompt to a real-life question.

Class Meeting 5

Have students sign up for COLOR groups and get their first LIT CIRCLE ROLE ASSIGNMENT.

Week 2

Students fill LIT CIRCLE roles. If it is not realistic in your school setting to assume all students can complete all assignments or homework, allot in-class time for reading. LIT CIRCLE roles work anyway.

Round	Red	Green	Purple	Orange	Blue
1	SUMMARIZER • Prepare a brief summary of today's reading to start group with 1 or 2 minute statements of key points, main highlights, and general idea of today's reading.	WORD WIZARD • Look out for 5-7 words that have special meaning in today's reading selection.	TRAVEL TRACER • Carefully track where the action takes place during today's reading. • Describe each setting in detail, either in words or with an action map or diagram.	ILLUSTRATOR • Draw some kind of picture related to the reading you have just done. • It can be a sketch, cartoon, diagram, flowchart, or stick-figure scene.	CONNECTOR • own past experiences • happenings at school or in the community • stories in the news • similar events at other times and places • other people or problems that you are reminded of between this book and other writings on the same topic or by the same author
2	CONNECTOR	SUMMARIZER	WORD WIZARD	TRAVEL TRACER	ILLUSTRATOR
3	ILLUSTRATOR	CONNECTOR	SUMMARIZER	WORD WIZARD	TRAVEL TRACER
4	TRAVEL TRACER	ILLUSTRATOR	CONNECTOR	SUMMARIZER	WORD WIZARD
5	WORD WIZARD	TRAVEL TRACER	ILLUSTRATOR	CONNECTOR	SUMMARIZER

Figure 1.1 Literature Circle Roles to enhance student engagement

Nine Yardsticks of Value

Teaching a general set of criteria early in the school year can help you build in latitude for honesty in your classroom. Introduce guidelines for evaluating and responding to literature that free students to write definitively about texts they do not like with as much confidence as about texts they thoroughly enjoy.

In English classes, middle school students generally look at literature in a quantitative way, learning elements of fiction—*characters, setting, plot, conflict, theme*, and so on—and may even have written some critical analyses. The next step is to look at literature in a qualitative way, thus developing a sounder and more defensible conclusion, seeing traits in literary works students may otherwise miss. Knowledge of such standards, in short, makes for thoughtful evaluations that will be more satisfying to students and more acceptable to their classmates. In these lessons, we will call these standards "yardsticks."

Consider adapting the *nine yardsticks of value* described in a literature text by Blair and Gerber. These educators suggest that students consider (1) clarity, (2) escape, (3) reflection of real life, (4) artistic details, (5) internal consistency, (6) tone, (7) personal beliefs, (8) emotional impact, and (9) significant insights. See figure 1.2 on which students can be asked to rate 1 to 5 (low to high) their evaluation of the reading. Then, they can talk and write based on their response to the text.

For the remainder of the course, invite students to use these criteria to consider the different genres and be prepared to quote or make a direct reference to examples from the beginning, middle, and end of the assigned reading. For example, if the class has read only three chapters during writing and discussion, students would draw evidence from those three chapters in support of their assertions about the text.

It may take two to three weeks to introduce all of the yardsticks, but doing so can help students

- see the sequential nature of their reading skills;
- discover reasons for their own responses to literature;
- expand their vocabulary for discussing and writing about texts; and
- read and analyze published literary criticism more insightfully.

all while becoming more open-minded, freer to write honestly, and willing to allow the creativity of the complex writer to draw them in, amaze, and inform them. Details of this approach are on the companion website for this book at www.teachingenglishlanguagearts.com.

Yardsticks of Value (Insert number to rate, low to high)	1	2	3	4	5	Page No. for Support
1. Clarity						
2. Escape						
3. Reflection of Real Life						
4. Artistry in Details						
5. Internal Consistency						
6. Tone						
7. Emotional Impact						
8. Personal Beliefs						
9. Significant Insights						

Figure 1.2 Nine Yardsticks of Value guide thinking about texts

VOCABULARY BEFORE, DURING, AND AFTER READING

Students should feel free to use the Internet as they read assigned texts. Model this for your students early in the course. Before they encounter them in the text, show students how to search for vocabulary words on the list you have prepared. Then click on "images" to demonstrate how both the denotation and various connotations of the words often appear. For English language learners this may be all they need to be able to read with more depth and understanding. For lifetime English speakers who read about a topic completely foreign to their experiences this tool will be equally helpful.

Learning the Language of the Land

You know the value of a broad, rich vocabulary, even if you just visit a different area of the nation and not some exotic country on a different continent. The same is true for your students. For many of them, the language of school may seem just as foreign to them. As you scope out the journey of the school year, you know students will need to understand some basic terms to be able to follow directions and stay on task. You can plan from the very beginning to teach vocabulary intentionally, without having to drill students just for them to acquire the skill of recognizing and using more sophisticated language in and out of class. If they use it, they won't lose it.

Consider levels of vocabulary. As you choose and prepare lessons around specific readings, select and provide definitions for words that are specific to that book/article. It also is expedient to pull out some of the published academic vocabulary students will need to know across the content areas. You may recognize these levels as tier 1, 2, and 3 words referring to the vocabulary based on how practical the words are for everyday speaking, reading, writing, and/or academic use. In your area of the country, you may hear about the 40/40/40 rule. Decide what words students need to know—for forty days, for forty weeks, for forty years—and then allot teaching and study time accordingly.

Displaying Vocabulary for Talking and Writing

Think about dedicating space for a word wall on which students see words daily during specific units and can refer to and draw from this word wall list when they write or talk about the literature. This can be a print or projected poster to which you add words throughout the course or one that you change to coordinate with specific units of instruction. On discussion or writing days, project a slide or draw students' attention to this word wall or poster to remind them to incorporate this vocabulary as they talk and write.

If space is available, it may be better to have one permanent poster with general words and a changing posting with specific words. Fresh lists create a new interest just as the changing road signs you notice along the highway revive an interest in the trip.

Among the academic words to begin defining and using in early lessons are those having to do with instructions: explain, diagram, evaluate, describe, analyze, discuss, and so on. If your students are new to middle school or new to academic work in English, they may have different ideas about what is required when asked to do these tasks. Help your travelmates get off to a good start by clarifying what is expected when they see or hear these terms. You can find lists of academic words on websites describing Bloom's Taxonomy Verbs to help you measure students' level of knowledge, comprehension, application, analysis, synthesis, evaluation, and creativity.

Once settled into your classes, you may want to present a lesson on the different definitions the same word may have in different content areas. Words like *plot* that in English is an element of fiction; in history/social studies' map reading may be a *plot* of land or *plot* a course of action; and in science or math—*plot* a graph, and so on. "Draw," as seen in the previous paragraph, is another of those multidefinition words. Then review those instruction terms in light of your course and give succinct examples of what you would expect to see when you assess their work.

Encouraging the Use of New Vocabulary

After vocabulary is taught, add using vocabulary words to customized rubrics. For example, when writing the final paper about a major work, include requirement to incorporate smoothly in their writing eight to ten vocabulary words from the recent vocabulary list.

Offer extra credit for using words from your vocabulary list in the graded writing they do for other courses—say, up to ten points (one point per word), turned in the week before the marking period ends. This due date will prevent your being overwhelmed recording extra credit work the week you have grades to calculate and submit for reports to parents and administration.

GETTING INTO THE READING

Are you familiar with the INTO, THROUGH, and BEYOND strategy for teaching text? Looking for something that can work in a single period to get students into their next book? Here are a few ideas to consider, keeping in mind that students from different cultures may respond differently but validly to these strategies.

Culture and Colors

Distribute your chosen book. Invite students to look carefully at the cover, front first, then back. Set your timer to ring after seventy-five seconds. Then have them turn and talk to partner about what they think the book will be about, just based on the graphics—images, colors, and fonts.

Allot time for a mini-lesson. Point out that colors have both positive and negative connotations as well as cultural differences. For example, red may mean warm love or cool hate; blue may mean loyalty or sickness; white in Western cultures usually means virgin purity, while in some Eastern cultures it's the color for death, worn by widows. Black in some cultures is worn by adult men to show power; in other cultures, black is reserved for preschool boys to show they have none yet.

You could just project a slide or distribute a handout or have students go to a site on their smartphones or tablets to explore quickly some of the meanings for different colors.

A Random Romp through the Book

Next, students should open their journals.

- Write any ten numbers from 1 to the last page number in the book.
- Turn to and skim those pages.
- Copy sentences from five of those pages that catch their attention because they seem:
  - interesting
  - surprising
  - provocative
  - confusing
- In a paragraph, write what they think these sentences say about characters, setting, or conflict or topic of this book.

Give the students a few minutes to share with one another their sentences and to talk briefly about similarities and differences in their inferences about the book. You may want to have them write in their journals and come back to them later to compare their before and after ideas about the book.

Resist the temptation to comment yourself. The goal here is to spark curiosity and inspire students to read to find answers.

Now, you do a dramatic read-aloud or play an audible version of the opening pages for five to seven minutes; stop and let students continue reading until five minutes before class period ends. During the final five minutes, give them an "exit slip" assignment to post or leave with you as they depart the classroom that asks question such as:

- What have you learned?
- What do you expect to happen next?
- What puzzles or confuses you?

If students have tech available, they can tweet or post to Padlet or whatever quick way you have taught them to respond with tech tools. Yes, they can write "exit slip" on scrap paper and hand it to you as they exit the room.

What usually happens is students continue reading, anticipating the sentences they copied and wondering if their inferences have been on or off target. Generally, once they begin, students will keep reading just to validate or expand their thinking.

In terms of quizzing, consider an open book option. One idea is to give students the option for their grade. Students can earn up to an A if they complete the quiz without using the book and a B maximum if they do.

Use Colors, Shapes, and Arrangements to Show Understanding

Another strategy you will see suggested in the chapters to come involves the use of colors and art. Students can demonstrate their understanding of character motivations, interactions, and relationships through color, shape, and arrangement as well as through sketching and diagramming.

About halfway through the book, assign something artsy that has them draw, chart, or diagram what they have been reading, and then share those with a small group. Yes, it probably will be evident that some are ahead or behind the assigned reading. Most will finish the reading on time.

If students have access to technology, you could have them use emojis to show the tone and emotions expressed by the author, and the mood and emotions experienced by the reader.

Consider this preparation lesson to get students thinking about colors and characters, colors and setting, colors and plot lines. Project and invite students to look closely at a painting, *Nine Colors* by Ellsworth Kelly, and think about the story you have just taught. Then, write in their own words the answers to the following questions:

- Which colors could represent the main characters? Quote lines from the text or make reference to specifics in the story to support your choice. Put the page numbers in parentheses. For example: Sylvia (Greenish circle), "When Lauren strolled into the restaurant in the same outfit as hers, Sylvia yelped with envy" (157); Lauren (Purplish circle), "She thinks she's a little princess" (182).
- Which colors could represent elements of setting: time and place?
- How would you rearrange the colored circles/squares to show the relationship among the characters? Which colors side by side? Which colors above or below another? Why? What words, phrases from story support your choices?
- How would you rearrange at least five of the colored circles/squares in a row to represent the events in the plot line? Arrange the colors from left to right.

If you decide to present this lesson in class, keep an open mind and allow students to use any colors and order they can validate with reasons. "I chose this color for this character because. . . . See, on page x, it says. . . ." As the school year unfolds, encourage students to use the literary terms you have taught as they verbalize their answers—out loud or in journals. For example, "I chose this color for the protagonist because. . . ," or "This is a good color for the opening lines in the exposition because. . ."

WRITING ABOUT LITERATURE

Students usually write well when they know what is expected. The challenge is to resist making the assignment so specific there is little room for creativity on their part. For this reason it is helpful to demonstrate that writing is a process during which students discover what they want to say and then, under teacher guidance and with peer feedback, learn how to say it better.

Since you, the teacher, have very definite skills you are asked to teach and must guide the students toward learning them and showing what they know about good writing, it may be useful to work backward by asking yourself questions like the following:

1. *What skills am I trying to develop or measure in this assignment?* Is it how well they understand the text they studied together, how well they can show what they know about analyzing a character, or how well they can write?
2. *What will I need to see in their writing to see and measure their level of understanding or skill?* Is it reference to the text? Is it use of literary language? Is it organization, development of ideas, correct use of vocabulary, grammar, and citations?

If it is all of these, plan a step-by-step lesson and do the following:

1. Ask students to review the literary language you have been teaching (direct/indirect characterization, motivation, elements of fiction, or whatever you have been teaching).
2. Ask students to work together and go back to the text to find examples of each of the devices/terms which they then save in their notes. Allow them to talk together and share their notes. As you listen to their talk, you gain insight into what they know or what you need to reteach.
3. Invite them to write a statement of their opinion about the topic you assign and have them use a modifier (adjective or adverb word, phrase or clause) to indicate their or your choice of

    - how well or poorly they think the author develops the characters;
    - how much the student identifies with the characters; or
    - how the student sees connections to everyday incidents in the way one or more characters act or react in the book.

Their essays will then be an attempt to show why that modifier is true/valid.

4. Then ask them to begin writing P.I.E. paragraphs in which they state their POSITION or opinion, next ILLUSTRATE with EXAMPLES from the beginning, middle, and end of the book, and then, EXPLAIN ways those

references support their position/opinion. Explaining is the most important element because it shows their level of understanding.
5. Then students will be ready to write introduction and conclusion paragraph's to lead into their paragraph(s) and reflect or summarize what they have written. Knowing there is no wrong answer, only unsupported ones, frees students to write eagerly and honestly.

- Rather than show them a fully polished sample essay, write along with them, demonstrating how you build your essay.
- Invite them to do an Internet search for words to describe writing.
- Generate a class list of responses from which they can choose their own modifier, or be free to select their own.
- Project your grading rubric that includes the minimum traits you expect to see in terms of content, organization, and correctness.
- Ask the students to reflect on their drafts, share them with partners to get feedback, revise, and then submit the papers for you to evaluate, using the same rubric you gave them when you gave the assignment.

Yes, this is a little formulaic, but it works well for less-confident students writing about their reading in this kind of essay. It also confirms for confident writers that they are on the right road to success in your course. Many eventually choose a pattern they like better that shows equally well what you need to see to assess their learning.

SAMPLE ORGANIZATION FOR IN-CLASS PEER RESPONDING

Writing class comments on classmates' draft. Find your name on the class list.

1. Skip THREE names on the list.
2. Upload the drafts of the next students.
3. Save to desktop with "Last Name—A," "Last Name—B," and "Last Name—C".
4. Insert comments into the draft according to the following guidelines.
5. At the end of the draft write one COMMENDATION and one RECOMMENDATION.

For Classmate A—Read and insert comments on general content.

Consider the body of the writing:

- best organization pattern
- variety of support information

Comment on strengths. Ask questions that arise as you read.

For Classmate B—Read and insert comments on general structure.

Consider the introduction:

- credibility mentioned?
- thesis/signpost?

Consider transitions within the body:

- Do they fit the organization pattern identified?
- Does the writer cite sources within the essay?

Comment on strengths. Ask questions that arise as you read.

For Classmate C—Read and insert comments on visual aids and references.

- Consider what and where the writer plans to use visual aids.
- Consider the quality and variety of the references.
- Does the writer cite sources within the outline?
- Check the domains.
- Correct the format (alpha order hanging indent).

Comment on strengths. Ask questions that arise as you read.

BUILD-IN LESSONS FOR STUDENTS TO MODEL WRITING IN DIFFERENT GENRES

Think about sports, music, and art. Who seems to appreciate a baseball game, an opera, or an unusual piece of abstract art? Usually it is a current or former athlete, musician, or artist. They know firsthand the skill and discipline it takes to play the game, make the music, or create the art. You can inspire respect for these authors by designing lessons for students to draft in various genres. As students experience writing in different genres, their level of understanding and enjoyment may even make them fans.

No, you do not have to make this a traditional creative writing class, but you can include assignments where students sample both the reading and the writing. For example, you could have students copy from their text into their journals three different sentences that help readers to visualize a person, a place, or an incident. Then during class, as students share their sentences, talk about ways syntax and vocabulary create images in the minds of the readers. Afterward, have the students pattern their favorite sentences, but write about something they have experienced, observed, or learned about in another course.

After studying short stories, assign students to draft one; do the same for poetry and drama. Once they have read, written, and talked about different genres and have also tried writing them, they will have a deeper appreciation for authors who write so well in those engaging genres.

MANAGING GRADING

While all the talking, using art, and writing is going on, you also have the responsibility to conduct assessments, not only to measure student learning but also to gauge your own teaching. Students, parents, and administrators want to know how you determine growth in your students. The sooner you decide how to communicate this, the more efficiently you will be able to construct lessons that reveal what you need to know and what students need to show that they are learning.

General Grading Guidelines

Establish your own set of general grading guidelines, perhaps based on the one in figure 1.3. Note that it simply says in order to earn a C on a process assignment (one on which students have time to get feedback and do revising), the document, product, or performance must be *complete*: includes the basic components of the assignments.

To earn a B, the product or performance should be *complete and correct*, having few distracting errors in MUGS for writing, sloppiness for performances. To earn an A, the writing or artwork, oral or video performance should be *complete*, *correct*, and *creative*, reflecting freshness in language, originality that is unexpected but effective, and revealing qualities that can only be acknowledged as something over and above completeness and correctness.

Customized Rubrics

A rubric, you recall, is a set of statements that identify traits on which something will be evaluated. According to Heidi Andrade's commonly accepted definition, the rubric can be for a document, product, or performance that articulates the expectations for an assignment by listing the criteria, or what counts, and describing levels of quality from excellent to poor. If your school or department does not have a general rubric for your course, consider the Six

GENERAL GRADING GUIDELINES

A = complete, correct, and creative
B = complete and correct
C = complete
D = deficient (something missing)
F = failing, for now

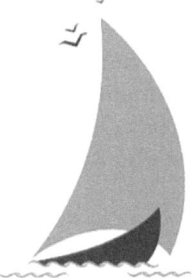

C = **THE SEA** – *Complete* (include all components of the assignment)
B = **THE BOAT** - Complete and *correct* (rides on the sea with minimal errors in mechanics, usage, grammar, and spelling)
A = **THE SAIL** - Complete, correct, and *creative* (something over and beyond the boat; original and fresh elements enhancing the final written paper, performance, digital or art product)

Figure 1.3   Share grading guidelines with students, parents, and administrators

Traits for Writing. The more recent version, Six Traits Plus One, has seven traits that include:

- ideas—the main message
- organization—the internal structure of the piece
- voice—the personal tone and flavor of the writer's message
- word choice—the vocabulary a writer chooses to convey meaning
- sentence fluency—the rhythm and flow of the language
- conventions—the mechanical correctness
- presentation—effective use of oral/visual media

Share this rubric with the class early in the course and then customize it for subsequent assignments, adding the specific elements or content expected on that assignment. For example, for *ideas/content* after having studied various literary devices, you may customize the assignment to say that to be complete, the student work must include examples from the reading that show three to five literary devices. Or, to be complete, the student must quote or reference examples from the beginning, middle, and end of the reading, or three different reliable online sources.

After teaching, modeling, and practicing a particular grammatical structure or style of referencing citations, you may customize the rubric *the sentence fluency* trait to indicate that to be complete and correct, the student work must include four different sentence beginnings. The *conventions* section could state that citations must be in Chicago style (or whatever style your school uses).

Customizing rubrics serves multiple purposes. The first is for you, the teacher. When you are preparing the assignment, you know what you need to see to measure learning, so include that on the rubric. Students need to know what they need to include to show that they know, so they can use the rubric to self-check their own work, and also to reference it when giving and receiving feedback from their peers. Even more critical, the customized rubric helps you align your testing with your teaching without teaching to the test.

Gradually Increase the Weight of Assignments

At the start of the year, big assignments (processed papers, projects, and presentations for which students have time to plan, get peer feedback, and revise) need not be weighted heavily enough to "kill" a quarterly grade. Similar high standards can be given for each assignment, but students have time to see the standards, get feedback on their performance, and seldom are so discouraged that they stop trying.

Say you plan about 500 points per marking period. Daily work completed on time earns full credit. Regular check-up quizzes graded in class by students can be worth 10–50 points. Both serve as practice for them and formative assessments for you. Use the general grading guidelines and customized rubrics, but give several opportunities to learn at low risk.

In the first quarter, you may give four short-process assignments: two written, one oral, and one art, but each is worth only thirty points. Like practice on a driving course, athletic team, orchestra, or choir rehearsal, students learn from their peers comments and grades from you. In the second quarter, you may give three such assignments, a little longer, but using the same basic rubric; in the third quarter, two such assignments; and in the fourth, a comprehensive summative assignment. This would be the main game or concert. For example:

- First quarter: Processed papers/projects/presentations = 30 points
- Second quarter: Processed papers/projects/presentations = 50 points
- Third quarter: Processed papers/projects/presentations = 75 points
- Fourth quarter: Processed papers/projects/presentations = 100 points

Let the Students Self-Grade

No, you will not be giving up control when you invite students to use the general grading guidelines and customized rubric to tell you what they think they earned. Instead, you are inviting them to reflect on their work and point out how their document, product, or performance demonstrates the grade they say they sought. The challenge for you will be to resist looking at their grades before you complete yours.

Have students send an e-mail or staple a folded note with their assignment. Hold on to these until you have completed the grading. Then, if the student's grade matches yours, raise that grade one half-step. C+ becomes a B-; B-, a B; B, a B+; B+ and an A-. It only takes three or four "rounds" before students begin grading themselves correctly. No need to change a grade if a student grades himself or herself lower; the comments on the grading sheet will show your reasoning for the higher grade. They will be pleased, and fewer students, parents, or administrators will challenge your grading. You will be pleased.

PLAN FOR INDEPENDENT READING

Build ways to encourage and support independent reading that will not punish students who do not choose to participate or burden you who must do the grading. Instead, consider a *contract*. Students decide how many books they think they can read during the marking period. Allot some in-class time for independent reading, especially if you teach a student body who is not likely to have time or space to read at home.

An initial survey can simply ask for their name, grade/course, date, kind of books they like to read, and the most recent book they have read. The contract, then, would ask them to plan ahead.

How many books can you read comfortably this next marking period to earn a C, B, or A? Which project will you plan to report on your independent reading?

- C = completed the number of books in the contract
- B = completed the number of books in the contract and turned in one of the required "reports" or presentations
- A = completed the number of books in the contract, submitted a required "report" or "presentation," and read one additional book on a different topic or by a different author

The independent reading project or report should be whatever you decide is an authentic way to assess the skills you have been teaching this marking period. It could be (1) a connection to what the whole class is reading, (2) something written, (3) artistic, (4) oral, (5) digital, (6) a one-on-one

Students sign an independent reading contract

conference, or one of the myriad creative assessments you know already, are learning here, and discovering elsewhere.

Making It Easy on Yourself

In the contract, students can simply list titles and authors of three books they plan to read during the coming marking period and indicate whether they plan to report in an oral, art project, or online media format. Then, by the week before the end of the marking period, students turn in or present their project. To save grading time for you, offer modest full credit for on-time projects. It will be the student's responsibility to sign up on the time you set for such reports.

Consider adding to your calendar class time for these presentations during week before official grading is due. Since students will be using class time and earning full credit, you should not have to plan in-class lesson for that day or have to allot at-home time for grading. You will have more time that final week to compute grades and write reports.

Having Student Audience Commit to Reading

Students in the class audience would be hearing about books they may consider reading the next marking period. To encourage their paying attention, have them fill out a feedback sheet checking off books they may read next time. Keep it simple. "I plan to read [title] this next marking period." Students turn these in to you at the end of the period either on paper or in response to an electronic query using an online app you have been using with them.

Whatever you decide for each marking period should offer student choice and be easy to grade. It's okay if during the next marking period new students give a report on book learned about from peers, as long as they give you a new report in a different form. Since the goal is to encourage independent reading and to have students practice English language arts (ELA) skills, just give the project modest weight and full credit for turning a report or project in on time. Not completing an independent reading contract should not fail a passing student.

PLAN TO BE FIRM, FAIR, AND FLEXIBLE

No matter how carefully teachers plan, something unexpected comes up in their students' lives that calls for acts of mercy. You can avoid seeming rigid with deadlines if you build in a safety net that does not increase the work load for you. One that has worked for many veteran educators is a *one-time-use late pass*.

During the first week of school, but not the first day, give students a printed or numerical late pass they can use once during the semester. This pass can be used to turn in the final document or product one class period late without losing credit. If the pass is not used, the late pass can be turned for credit before the expiration date set one week before the marking period ends. The credit can be ten points or whatever the late penalty would have been.

The value in this late pass policy is that its use need not disrupt your teaching and grading. Few teachers can grade all final documents (written papers) or products (art or media projects) in just a few days, so having one come in late usually does not extend the grading time as much a receiving one poorly done. Having students earn extra ten points during a marking period will probably just make up for a quiz grade earned when the student was unprepared.

Most presentations, however, are scheduled during class time, and being late for one of those could be disruptive. For that reason, it may not be wise to include that in the late pass program. If, on the other hand, the presentation is electronic and you and students can view it at another time, that assignment may be eligible for late pass credit. You decide what will be fair, and no more work for you.

Full Credit for On-Time Preliminary Steps and Self-Reflection

Plan grading that assigns full credit for on-time early steps and gives students fewer reasons to get too far behind. For example, on a multiple-step assignment leading to a heavily-weighted document, project, or performance, consider the following for a 100-point assignment:

- 10 points for written plan/outline
- 15 points for on-time first draft
- 15 points for written courteous, constructive feedback to peers
- Up to 50 points for on-time final document, product, or performance (based on grading rubric)
- 10 points for on-time self-reflection and grading

Considering the time and purpose of grading will help you adapt this approach to fit the assignments you design and the school population you teach. Keep in mind, building in flexibility makes it less stressful to be firm, and you will be viewed as a fair teacher who understands the reality of being a student. More important, you will reduce the stress on yourself. Most important, you and your students remain on the road to success with your teaching and their learning.

Circulate, observe, and assist as needed

LEARNING FROM TESTS

Young and inexperienced students still are learning how to take tests and how to learn from the kinds of mistakes they make. So it is useful to schedule in your overall plans full-class meetings to prepare students to take those comprehensive assessments and then another class meeting to go over tests when you return them.

On those post-test days, you could ask students to come with their self-selected reading books. If you finish your test analysis early, the students can begin or continue reading on their own in preparation for the next quarter book report. This independent reading time can be an opening to meet privately with the few students who may have done more poorly on the assessment than you or they expected. Often it will have been a minor issue that caused a major loss of points.

Reflecting on Errors Leads to Fewer

What kinds of topics should you cover during test analysis? First, ask the students to determine the kinds of errors they made. Did they make errors because of

- misreading the question or prompt;
- running out of time;
- misunderstanding a concept, term, or instruction;
- studying the wrong material;
- failing to respond to the question;
- missing clues to answers in the prompt or stem of multiple-choice questions; and/or
- others issues?

Once the students determine the kinds of errors they made, talk about ways to avoid them on the next test. Usually, the learners calm down when they see that correcting one problem before the next test can help them miss fewer points on the next assessment.

Analyzing Tests Can Lead to Student Confidence

You may spend time talking about ways to develop confidence that they are answering questions correctly. One way is to have students underline the verb that tells them what to do and put a rectangle around the direct object, the noun indicating what they should be looking for or working on. If they cannot write on the test/quiz, you may ask the students to write those key words on edge of their answer sheet. Taking a few minutes to do something physical helps the test-takers to focus on what is being asked of them.

If there has been vocabulary on the test, invite students to point out the clues in the sentences that could have helped them know they had chosen the correct response. For example, some sentences may have a synonym, an antonym, or a definition in the prompt question. As students learn to look for such clues, they are more likely to recognize the correct answers.

One of your additional tasks as a teacher is to help students develop better reading strategies and more efficient test-taking skills. Taking the time to do this immediately after administering the first few tests/quizzes is sure to reap positive benefits for both students and teachers.

You are happier when students do well on your assessments. You also want to learn whether the assessments you plan actually reveal what you have taught. If, during analyses with the students, you discover they are missing questions you were sure they would be able to handle easily, you may find it necessary to revise your questions or rework the layout of the tests/quizzes you administer.

Guiding Students to Prepare for Tests

It also is important to develop tests that ask students to show what they know in a variety of formats—multiple-choice, matching, true/false, paragraph writing, or short essay. This can be done incrementally. Early in the school year, design tests that include questions requiring factual information in the first couple of sections, and then follow with prompts for short answer responses. Those "fact questions" trigger students' memories.

By the time they get to the sections that necessitate longer answers requiring them to show ability to interpret and connect facts to other literature or life, students usually feel confident they can handle this higher-level thinking. Depending on the skills development of the students in a particular year, you can reserve fact questions for interim quizzes, and on tests focus questions that require full sentence, paragraph, or essay responses.

CONCLUSION

Now that you have laid the ground work, strap on your seatbelts and get ready for the ride. Along the way, you will have time to refuel your tanks with more ideas for

- managing grades;
- assessing understanding informally and formally;
- teaching vocabulary for reading;
- writing about and in response to reading; and
- using a variety of means to show understanding.

as you teach the different genres generally taught in basic ELA courses. You can add to your tank the energy and inspiration for the miles to come.

NOTE

1. Rudine Sims Bishop, *Good Reads*. https://www.goodreads.com/author/quotes/170243.Rudine_Sims_Bishop (accessed July 26, 2018).

Chapter 2

Unpacking the Story and Understanding the Genre

The best of my English teachers taught us literature because they wanted the art of it to expand our minds and help teach us new ways of seeing the world. I was taught to both see a work of literature as a way to understand the time it was written, and the people who produced it, and to find the parts of that work that spoke to me in my time and place.[1]

—Sybylla Yeoman Hendrix

You can adapt ideas from this chapter to design lessons to introduce students to the basic elements of fiction by reading short stories, and analyzing plot structures and characterization. You may even decide to allot time for coaching students to compose their own short story to submit to a school journal or to publish online. As readers learn the language of literature and come to appreciate how the elements work to construct stories, they also begin seeing themselves and the world in new ways.

In much the same way that veteran world travelers learn some of the basic words or phrases for countries they will visit enabling them to read signs, navigate new territory, and enjoy the trip, your challenge is to teach the language of literature without diluting that appreciation.

At the same time, as a professional you know you must also develop and present lessons that help your students meet your school, district, or state standards for the English language arts. Your lessons should likely include close reading, making logical inferences and citing specific textual evidence in speaking and writing to support conclusions drawn from the text.[2]

INTRODUCING THE ELEMENTS OF FICTION

Here is a way to get started. Students need a journal, a spiral notebook, or an electronic device to which they have daily access. This study aid can be taken home daily, but if more appropriate for your school setting, set up boxes or bins to store these notebooks on classroom shelves. Then students can pick up their journals at the beginning of each class meeting and return them at the end. You could set timer to ring five minutes before the end of class time to summarize the day's lesson, allow time to write or post questions as exit slips, mention upcoming assignments, then have students pack up and return, in an orderly way, their notebooks or tablets to the appropriate box or bin.

To help maintain order, label the bins or boxes with the class period number and sections of alphabet. If students have access to computers in the classroom every day, help the youngsters set up electronic files and folders they can access easily. Show them the link on the school server and age-appropriate online sites you have vetted that connect them to a safe place to save their files so they can access them in class, on the school site, or at home.

Setting Up Student Journals

To start a series of lessons, ask students to set up their own journal section for short stories by folding a page in half vertically, forming a half-page bookmark titled "short stories" or creating a digital folder for this purpose. So begins their own story in this unit—the opening of their files or turning of their page (not a bad metaphor!). Every new life story is a chance to begin again.

Then ask students to write on the next clean page in their journals the current date in the upper-right-hand corner, and, as you introduce them, the elements of fiction on the top line. Remind the students that all writers start with blank pages even if they use computers. Few students ever think about the fact that most of what they read for your class was first written or sketched out on paper, typed on a typewriter, or word-processed on a computer.

Next, point out to your students that writers use proven techniques to engage readers—just as musicians use notes, chords, and rhythms. Few published authors write just to quickly express themselves—as many bloggers do. Knowing the different facets of fiction helps writers write, and readers read. In fact, understanding the structure of literature can assist in all kinds of human communication, from interviewing for a job to making a movie.

Normally it is best to teach those literary terms that are included in your course textbook. If the text does not define terms, you can use the ones that follow, or write your own in words, phrases, and terms designed for your own students. Consult reliable Internet sites to refresh yourself with different definitions; find brief explanations and examples for each of the terms.

Many of the lessons here follow the same basic order:

- Teach or demonstrate the literary term (an element of fiction).
- Assign reading a story that clearly illustrates the term.
- Encourage students to pay attention to ways the story reflects the elements.
- Invite students to read for fun so they do not focus so much on identifying the elements that they fail to enjoy the story.
- Assign several stories quickly, since multiple examples can be more effective than one that the students miss on the first read.

Assess Students' Prior Knowledge

You may decide to do a pretest to discover what terms your students already know. If so, simply create a list of terms they are expected to know by the end of the school year. Distribute the list and ask them to put a star next to the terms they know and can explain, a check next to the terms they recognize, and a minus sign next to the terms that are completely new to them. If they are working on electronic devices, have them change font color to green to the words they know; to purple to the words they recognize, and red to the terms that are totally new to them.

Allot in-class time for independent reading

As students are marking the lists, circulate, peeking over their shoulders to see if you notice a pattern among terms starred (green) and checked (red). When you see most have completed this step, set timer for three or four minutes for students to turn and talk to a partner, explaining to their peer the words they starred and their partner checked. Again, listen as they talk. Students usually see they have more knowledge than they imagined, but still have much to learn. Commend them for their candid responses and helpful conversations. Collect or save their lists, tally the results, and decide how best to use this formative assessment to adjust upcoming lessons.

Remember, it is always appropriate to review. Then, if students already know many of the basic terms, you may just speed up the pace of the lessons that follow.

Assign Optional or Required Book Report

You may find this a good time to assign a book report or project for quarter one. Allot a class period to visit the library to locate and check out books, and regularly schedule in-class time to read them. Sometimes a special side trip during a tour is just the thing to re-energize those committed to a long trip.

These self-selected books also provide fine fodder for feeding their minds, expanding their understanding about ways authors use the literary devices you are teaching. These books also provide a getaway for some students who need respite from the challenges of their personal and academic lives. See chapter 1 for ideas for assigning independent reading.

Lesson One: Plot

1. Ask students to turn to the short story section of their notebooks or electronic journals. Explain that stories are about characters faced with solving a problem or confronting a conflict. The first term—*Plot* or narrative arc—is the series of events that make up a story. Plot usually includes six parts: exposition, triggering action, rising action, climax, falling action, and resolution.
2. Draw a diagram of a plot line on the board or use one prepared on a poster or for a slide to project. See your class anthology or an online source for sample plot line or story arc. (See figure 2.1.)
3. Fill in the six parts of the plot line as you explain the function of each part:

    - *Exposition*: Introduces the main characters, setting, conflict, and point of view. (Ex = out, position = places. Exposition = places out for the reader)
    - *Triggering action*: That story point when the main character decides to do something about the problem confronted in the exposition.

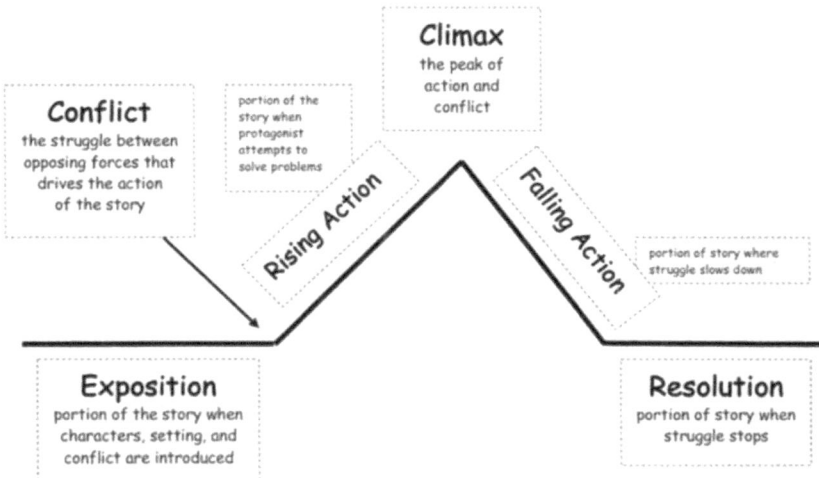

Figure 2.1 Plot diagrams help student visualize story structure

- *Rising action*: A series of events during which the main character attempts to solve the problem laid out in the exposition. Usually there are three attempts:
  - the first very simple attempt, often by protagonist alone
  - the second more difficult, often requiring the help of another character
  - the third most complex, often requiring the main character to make a moral or ethical decision
- If students are familiar with classic fairy tales, ask them to consider how often this three-part rising action occurs—"Three Little Pigs," "Goldilocks and the Three Bears," "Three Billy Goat's Gruff," and so on. Ask for examples of stories with which they may be more familiar in their culture or language; consider storylines from movies or TV shows.
- *Climax*: The highest point of suspense in the story, when the reader, viewer, or listener wonders whether the main character has gotten into such trouble that he or she cannot get out. But then the turning point occurs, and the reader can see (happily) that the problem can be solved or (tragically) that the character has given up or been permanently overcome.
- *Falling action*: The issues raised during the rising action begin to fall into place, the complications of the rising action seem to unravel, and

the action begins to wind down. Some texts call this the dénouement (day-noo-mon).
- *Resolution*: The action stops. Readers see the main character either has solved the problem or given up (not all stories have happy endings).

Add Plotline Sound Effects

Talking about a plotline is not nearly as engaging as telling the story itself. Therefore, it helps students to make your plotline mini-lesson into a story by adding appropriate sound effects. After all, over 50 percent of the emotional impact of a movie is the soundtrack. If you have software like PowerPoint, create a diagram of a plotline in which each step in the plot appears on the screen with appropriate sound effects. The "transition" feature in PowerPoint allows you to vary the effects and their loudness.

This activity can also serve as a course project using images. Consider making or adding the sounds a roller-coaster car emits as it begins, ascends, lurches at the top, descends, and then slows at the end of the ride. Do whatever it takes to make the lesson interesting for you and memorable for students.

Model Noticing Plot Elements

Reading a short story aloud and asking students to raise their hands when they recognize an element is a way to focus their attention on the elements, and also a no-stress assessment for you to determine whether they "get it." But be sure to stop reading at a critical plot point, to entice the students to continue reading the story themselves just to find out what happens next.

Close the session giving the reading assignment, asking students to identify the narrative arc and plot parts in the story you assign. Encourage, but do not require, them to draw and label the plot line in their journals. If you are teaching with block-scheduling, you can use the additional time to start or complete a short story in class, and provide time for students to talk together, identifying parts of the plot.

Lesson Two: Conflict

In fiction, conflict is the problem the main character(s) must resolve as a result of a struggle against opposing forces. The main character may face internal conflict—a struggle for dominance between two elements within a person—or external conflict or conflict when the character struggles against an outside force—often both.

Once you introduce the topic of conflict, students should be ready to work in pairs for ten minutes to identify plot elements in the story they have just

Unpacking the Story and Understanding the Genre 31

read. They can work together, referring to the definitions they wrote in their notebooks and identifying specific examples from the text.

Since sharing desk space is a psychological reminder to students that they are sharing what they are learning, it is appropriate to encourage them to collaborate by pulling their desks together and talking with one another. Circulate during discussions to learn

- what students recall about the previous day's lesson and from the story they just read;
- what needs to be re-taught or clarified before continuing the lesson; and
- who has and has not done the homework.

Next, lead a classroom discussion of student conclusions for about fifteen minutes. This discussion/response format reveals that there is often more than one right response to a question, especially in the study of literature. Also, it allows you to determine students' understanding of the material and readiness for formal assessment. Finally, this format is an excellent practice for writing fully developed essays. You may recognize it as the P.I.E. structure in which students made a POINT, use examples to ILLUSTRATE their point, then EXPLAIN the link between the two.

Model P.I.E. Format to Show Students Possible Responses

- *State an opinion:* "I think that the climax of 'The Three Little Pigs' is when the wolf comes down the chimney."
- *Support that opinion* with an example from the text: "On page three it says, 'Finally, the wolf got so hungry that he jumped down the chimney.'"

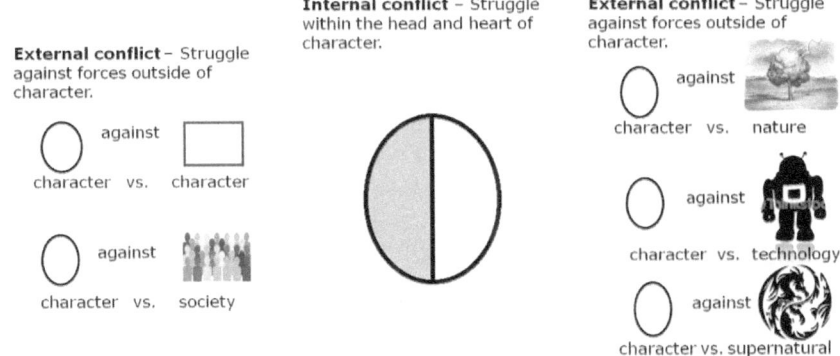

Figure 2.2 Conflict may be internal, external, or both

- *Explain how* the chosen passage illustrates the definition of the term: "This seems like the high point of the story because the reader really wonders if the pigs will be okay. Also, the action of the story starts to fall after this happens."

Invite students who diagramed the plot line of this story to share with those seated near them.

Two Kinds of Conflict (figure 2.2)

Internal conflict occurs when a character struggles within himself or herself to decide what is the right, moral, or safe action. It is something like the cartoon of the devil and angel sitting on opposite shoulders of a character, trying to persuade the character to take certain actions.

External conflict occurs when the main character struggles against forces outside of himself or herself. The students may need to be reminded that even an animal or alien protagonist demonstrates a human-like struggle. Examples of external conflict are

- *person versus person*—struggle is with another character
- *person versus nature*—struggle is against a force of nature—weather, thirst, illness, or topography (desert, mountain, roiling rapids)
- *person versus society*—struggle is against a group of people acting as one—a team, racial group, pack of peers, political party, social club, or ethnic tribe, and so on
- *person versus technology*—struggle is against a machine, like a car, tractor, tank, android, or computer that may occur in real life or science fiction
- *person versus the supernatural*—struggle is against a ghost, an alien, the gods, or a Supreme Being as may be seen in myths, religious or fantasy fiction

Discussing Conflict

Ask students to identify the conflict in the story they just completed and reply using P.I.E. response structure. Encourage them to include transition "because" statements to clarify their answer, illustrate it with an example from the text, and explain why that example fits the definition of the term they have just studied. Yes, insisting on P.I.E. talk may slow down the rate of responses, but P.I.E. necessitates deeper thinking and your requiring it allows for those who process information more slowly the time to do so. And, skeptics may be open to other ideas when they hear their classmates' rationales.

Assign another short story for homework. If time permits, read aloud the opening passages. This often is enough to hook the students, and they are more likely to complete the reading on their own. For this reading, ask all the students to draw a plot line, one that represents the relative length of time it takes for each section of the story to unfold.

Some stories have long expositions and precipitous falling action and minimal resolutions; others may be just the opposite. Let the shape of the plot line show that relationship. "The Most Dangerous Game," by Richard Connell is an excellent choice for illustrating the types of conflict and an interesting plot structure. Ask students to label the incidents in the rising action. This can be fun for them and you to see how consistent they are in identifying those events of plot.

Lesson Three: Setting

The setting of a story is the time and place in which the action occurs. In a short story, the setting is particularly limited—sometimes just a single day or a few hours and in a single location. Here is a suggested schedule for engaging students in a review of what you have taught and an introduction to this other basic element of story structure:

1. For ten minutes, review the elements of plot in the story the students just read. Ask them to work in pairs to identify the elements and the kind(s) of conflict.
2. Conduct a ten- to fifteen-minute, full-class discussion for students to share observations about the new story. This can be a think-pair-share format, or just turn and talk. It's important to build in time for students to talk, using the terminology you are teaching and have projected in a list they can see as they talk.
3. For the remaining time, guide the students through these new definitions:

    Setting in terms of time

    - Time of day: dawn, morning, afternoon, evening, night
    - Time of year: winter, spring, summer, fall
    - Time of life: childhood, teen years, adult, old age
    - Time in history: prehistoric, medieval, Elizabethan Age, future

    Setting in terms of place

    - Area of place: inside, outside, porch, roof, basement, or cellar
    - Locale: city, country, mountains, sea, valley, forest
    - Continent: Africa, Asia, Europe, North or South America
    - Galaxy: Earth, another planet, another galaxy

4. Finally, assign a new short story to read and ask students to pay close attention to the ways the author establishes setting. Ask them to consider

how the setting makes them feel or creates a mood. Wait until the next period to remind them of the typical impact of daytime versus nighttime when good or bad things happen, rural versus urban places when the characters may be relaxed versus tense. Depending on the students, the responses to these locations may be inverted. Some are more comfortable in the country and very tense in the city.

Interacting with Text Slows Down Reading but That's Okay

If students are permitted to write in their textbooks, ask them to pencil-in rectangles around words or phrases that reveal setting and then write "T" in the margin for "time" and "P" in the margin for "place." If the students are not permitted to write in their books, ask them to keep notes in their journal or use sticky notes.

This active response to reading affirms what they are learning or reminds them about what they need to ask about during the next class meeting. Those using e-texts that allow it can insert comments or highlight to show this element of fiction. Encourage students to complete the story first, then go back and label elements. Stopping while they are reading can disrupt the flow of the story and cause students to miss something important.

Lesson Four: Characters—Act I

Fictional characters: (1) play roles in the story and (2) are developed to different degrees. The main character or *protagonist* usually solves the problem set forth in the exposition of the story. The *antagonist* is the opposing person (personal) or opposing force (impersonal). Authors create *static* or *dynamic*, *flat* and/or *round* characters, and reveal characters' personalities and motivations through *direct* and *indirect* means. As before, consider this schedule for the day's topic:

1. Have students work in pairs for ten to fifteen minutes on the homework, discussing ways the author used setting in the previous day's story. Note vivid language that creates mental pictures. You could ask them to describe how they feel (the mood) using colors to symbolize those feelings. Be alert to cultural differences related to what specific colors may mean.
2. Then conduct a P.I.E. class discussion, encouraging the students to use the literary vocabulary and to back up their views with specific passages from their texts. Remind class members to turn to the pages as their peers reference them. Seeing the passage again will help them recall details when called upon to write or take a test.
3. Introduce the topic of characters. Show or reproduce diagrams of characterization. (See for example, figure 2.3.)

Characters: People who are faced with solving a problem in a story. (Could be animals acting as humans.)

Flat: one dimensional, predictable, one-sided character

Round: one reader learns more about as story progresses

Static: does not change as the story progresses

Dynamic: changes as a result of involvement in the conflict

Figure 2.3 Different kinds of characters

4. List the main characters on the board and use them to review the basic literary terms already introduced. You could use colors here to represent personalities of characters.

Be sure to remind students to write lecture-discussion notes in their journals to supplement the definitions, because knowledge of key concepts will be quizzed soon and tested later.

Distinguishing Kinds of Characters

Some notes about characters:

- The *protagonist* is a human or other human-like character who struggles to overcome conflict. Suspense develops as readers get to know more about the protagonist's motivation, personality, and the ways the protagonist responds to obstacles.
- The *antagonist* is the opposing force (external forces include another character, a group, nature, technology, or even supernatural forces; internal forces refer to the conscience).
- *Characterization* describes how authors reveal characters' personalities and motivations. Authors reveal such traits and motives directly or indirectly.

Here is a direct, expressed motive about the character "Claude": "Claude is a popular guy but is feared by most of the students in the school." If the author merely has other characters shrink away from, and steer clear of Claude, then readers can infer characters in the story are afraid of Claude, even though the readers are not told so directly in a statement by the author.

Identifying Characterization Strategies

After introducing or reviewing the specifics about characters, ask students to identify the kinds of characterization the authors have used in stories read so far. Set timer for them to meet in groups around a chosen story and plan a two-minute report of specific examples in the text to support their responses. Encourage them to talk among themselves as they search for text clues.

Once again, circulate among them, listening to their reasoning and assessing insight into their level of understanding. Set a low-volume notification tone to alert groups when two minutes is up, but do not stop them in mid-sentence. Do the same for group report-outs. At the end of the session, summarize the terms and assign a new story.

Lesson Five: Characters, Act II

Character development is complicated and involves an additional day of study. Explain how some characters develop and change as the story unfolds. One option is to ask students why people do something right or wrong. The point is everyone is complex; people act on the basis of mixed motives. Real "characters" are not simple. In this regard, more complex fictional characters are like readers—and readers are like them. Show or reproduce the diagram on characters and explain that for fictional purposes, authors use a range of character types:

> *Dynamic* and *static* characters: Usually the protagonist is a dynamic character who changes as a result of attempting to solve the conflict. Most minor characters are static; they change very little or not at all.

> *Round* and *flat* characters: Round characters learn more as the story progresses but might not change (blowing up a balloon changes its shape, but not its basic nature). Flat characters are usually one-dimensional (like a paper doll), static, and often stereotypical (e.g., the pudgy best friend, the sidekick, the shy and bespectacled nerd, the bully, and the trickster or fairy tale's evil stepmother). See www.teachingenglishlanguagearts.com, the companion website for this text, for sample slide presentation on characterization.

This is the good stopping point for introducing new literary terms; have students review each term referencing all previous stories for examples. Then assign a more challenging story with more fully developed characters and a more complex plot. Edgar Allen Poe's short stories often fit this description but may be challenging for younger students or those inexperienced reading in English. Later lessons are designed to introduce more literary devices. You could use "The Most Dangerous Game" here, or one that represents the cultural heritage of your students.

Differentiating Instruction

Now that you know your students better, it may be an appropriate time to differentiate your instruction. Set up groups of four or five students based on common interests or reading levels. Guided by what you have learned about your students so far, assign the groups to read different stories from the anthology. If it suits your situation, two groups can read the same story. Consider assigning literature circle roles described in Chapter One.

Observing and Noting Who's Learning

During the next class meetings, those who have read the same stories could meet in small groups to discuss their findings using the vocabulary of literature they are learning. Again, observe, listen, and take notes on: (1) who is confident using the new terms; (2) who finds accurate examples to validate their claims about the story; (3) who is encouraging and supportive;(4) who sits and listens first, but responds with comments that show they know what is going on; and (5) who hasn't a clue. All this anecdotal information can help you plan the next set of lessons tailored to meet the dynamics and learning styles of students you currently are teaching.

Lesson Six: Point of View

Point of view (POV) is the perspective from which an author tells a story. The various points of view include:

- *First-person POV*: The author writes as though he or she is a character inside the story. The author, writing as the character, uses first-person pronouns and comments on his or her own thoughts and feelings about the incidents in the plot. For example, if Charles Dickens had written his classic story about Scrooge as though he, Dickens, were the character, Scrooge, the reader would know only what Scrooge sees and hears, thinks and does. With the limitations of first-person POV, the reader would not know what has gone on in Tiny Tim's house before Scrooge arrives.
- *Objective or third-person POV*: The author writes the story as though he or she is outside the story: limited to listening and observing what characters

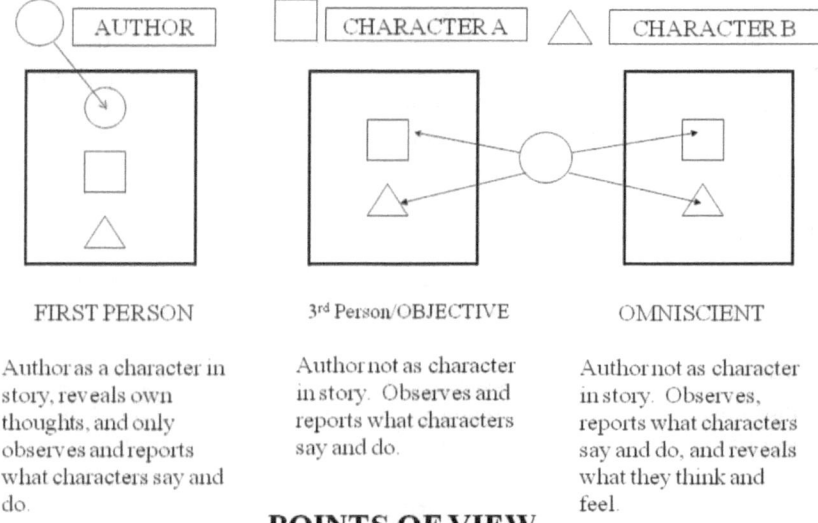

POINTS OF VIEW
Diagram adapted from work of Blair and Gerber, 1959

Figure 2.4

say and do—like a reporter. The author uses third-person pronouns (he, she, they—not we or I) to report the speech and actions of the characters in the story.

The objective POV offers a broader perspective than the first-person POV because the author stands outside of the story and can observe characters in different settings. The characters can speak in the first person, but the author is reporting on their speech. Speaking frankly, you know that no writing is completely objective because the author's attitude (tone) always shines through the choices of words, images, structure, and time spent on the topics. But, for purposes of introducing POV, this term can suffice.

- *Omniscient POV*: The author writes the story as though he or she is outside the story but can also see into the hearts and minds of the characters inside the story. The author not only listens and observes what characters say and do, but also relates what these characters think and feel, like an all-knowing Supreme Being. The author not only uses third-person pronouns, but also words like "ponders, senses, feared, and worried" to show the inner thoughts and feelings of the characters. This is the broadest POV because the author gets inside the heads and hearts of the characters and can comment on their thoughts and feelings as the story progresses.
- *Limited omniscient POV*: An author limits the revelation of thoughts and feelings to just one character, often the protagonist. To understand this,

imagine being able to read the mind of one of your friends, but not the mind of a different friend. This is the way Dickens wrote *A Christmas Carol*. The reader knows what Scrooge is thinking and feeling, but can infer that information about other characters only based on what they say and do.

Showing Point of View with Four Geometric Shapes (figure 2.4)

- As you draw a circle on the board, identify it for the students as the author, a rectangle to represent the book (story), a triangle for one character, and a square for a second character.
- For first-person POV: Draw a rectangle and to the left, a circle. Next, inside the rectangle, draw a triangle and square. Add a circle inside. Then, draw an arrow from the circle outside the circle to the one inside to show the author is writing as a character inside the story. Let the arrow pierce the inside circle to show the author reveals inner thoughts and feelings.
- For objective or third-person POV: Draw the same rectangle, with circle outside and a triangle and square inside. Draw arrow from circle to edge, but not inside the triangle and square to show the author is writing as an observer, choosing not to reveal those inner thoughts and feelings.
- For omniscient POV: Draw the same graphic as for objective POV, except this time draw arrows from the outside circle to inside the triangle and square to show this author can also reveal what characters think and feel.
- For limited POV: Same diagram, but arrow only pierces inside the triangle, to show author reveals what only one of the characters thinks and feels.

Have students copy the diagram in their reading journals as a reference for later.

After reviewing previously taught literary terms with students, help them identify each author's point of view in the works the class has already read. Ask them to consider how each author's story would have been different if it were told from another point of view. What would the readers be able to know and when? What impact does that perspective have on the story? Student comments usually vary but should indicate the limitations of first and objective points of view and perhaps the different level of suspense created with omniscient point of view.

Helping Students Picture Point of View—Shoot It!

Perhaps no contemporary media genre illustrates point of view better than the news. Modern news is not just factual; someone has to decide what to report, how to cover it, whom to interview, what to include in the final copy, and images or sounds. During the week that you're introducing the concept of point of view, ask interested students in groups of two or three to "cover" a school sports event with a digital camera, using no more than three photos and thirty seconds of "copy" to summarize the game.

As long as at least two groups participate they should be able to compare the points of view of different reporter-editors as they read their copy and show their images to the class. *Hint*: Don't tell them in advance whether to use any first-person or objective copy in describing the event. See what they come up with on their own.

WRITING ABOUT SHORT STORIES

Once you complete this series of lessons, it is a good time for a stress-free writing assessment that follows up discussion. Continue your focused observation as students work independently, then in small groups, and finally as a whole class. Here is an idea to guide students in summarizing a story in three to five sentences using the basic journalistic questions: who, what, when, where, why, and how? First, model this way to glean specific information from a story:

- Who?—List main characters—protagonist and antagonist(s)
- What?—List seven to ten verbs that identify plot events. For example, choose a common fairy tale (or movie). Ask the students to list verbs, using only the verbs for "Little Red Riding Hood," "Goldilocks and the Three Bears," or a different, but well-known, tale. Goldilocks:

  1. walks
  2. sees
  3. peeks
  4. tastes
  5. sits
  6. sleeps
  7. awakens
  8. fears
  9. flees

- When?—When does the action occur—or from when to when?
- Where?—Where does the majority of the action take place?
- Why?—Why do the protagonist and antagonist act the way they do?—What drives or motivates them to act? You could offer vocabulary for motivation like fear, love, hunger, hate, power, greed, jealousy, or a sense of adventure.
- How?—How do the main characters accomplish their deeds—physically, mentally, both? How does the author reveal character motivation? How does the author use setting to create a mood?

Unpacking the Story and Understanding the Genre 41

Allot time for students to turn and talk about texts

After using these prompts to gather the basic reportorial story information, together with the students assisting with wording, write a three- to five-sentence summary paragraph, so they get the idea.

Next assemble students into brainstorming groups to gather facts (in 8–10 minutes) about one of the stories they just read for class. Two groups can work on the same story, as needed. Tell them that they are to report their findings to the rest of the class. When someone from each group reports to the rest of the class, point out that groups sometimes identify different Ws or Hs in their reports. Be open with students about the fact that different interpretations can be correct because stories and their characters are often complex—unlike simplistic TV commercials or cartoons with stereotypical characters.

After group brainstorming, have students work independently for five to seven minutes or so writing their own summaries. Conclude the period by having one student from each group read his or her summary aloud while the rest of the class decides whether each reader has included all six requirements. What's missing? Who can add the missing information?

This reportorial activity provides a good appraisal of the class's readiness for a test or quiz on literary terms and story elements. If the students are ready, give them a test or quiz in a day or so. If not, take a couple more days to work with simpler stories and to practice identifying elements and using text evidence to support opinions and observations. Skills developed here writing summaries about short stories come in handy when you teach students how to conduct research and want them to write summaries of their findings.

DIGITIZING STUDENT OBSERVATIONS

What fun! Collaborate, review, produce, reinforce, decorate, learn, and teach with online cloud generators. For a whole class, in small groups, or as individuals, you can invite students to use online generators like a cloud on websites like tagxedo.com or wordclouds.com to create artwork reflecting student responses to reading. (See figure 2.4.)

Ask the students to write a paragraph describing a character, summarizing the events in a scene, discussing the theme of a novel or play, highlighting the main ideas in an essay, or critiquing a movie, and then make the cloud.

Figure 2.4 Word clouds reveal key/repeated words in larger fonts

Unpacking the Story and Understanding the Genre 43

But, as recommended, model this activity. Make a class cloud by having the students write one of the following:

- ten words describing one of the main characters;
- one sentence summarizing a recently read scene from the literary work;
- one sentence stating in their own words one of the main ideas in the story; or
- one sentence critiquing the literary work.

Then in groups of five, invite the students to post their group's lists (keep duplicate words so that each cloud represents all fifty words), or all the sentences into one of the cloud text screens. Next, generate, print, or project this class cloud. If reviewing a longer work or play, divide the book into chapters or sections, or for a play into scenes or acts, and let students sign up for their preferred scenes. Remember, the more times a single word appears in the text, the more prominently it will appear in the cloud. That's the point.

Create a class collage of all the group clouds. This should make for an interesting visual summary of what the students are thinking, observing, concluding. When these word clouds are posted, recurrent words and phrases will highlight and thus reinforce the key observations.

APPLYING NEWLY LEARNED SKILLS: BOOK REPORT #1

The end of the first quarter is a great opportunity to have students independently apply what they are learning about the elements of fiction, but in a text they are reading on their own. If it is not realistic to expect your students to complete a book outside of class, allot twenty minutes daily for the next couple of weeks for them to read in class. To make efficient use of class time, set up a schedule so that all students study grammar and sentence structures for about half the period and read independently the remainder of the period, preparing for the assignment of their choice.

Using Independent Reading Book to Teach Grammar

During these two weeks, invite students to refer to their independent reading books for examples of the grammatical and sentence structures you are teaching. They can practice the grammar being learned by writing about their own books. You can make that determination based on the grade and skill level of the students as revealed in the writing you already have seen them do on earlier assignments.

An end-of-semester book report asks students to make connections between the story in their self-selected work of fiction and the stories they have studied together in class. It can also include a speech component to get them acclimated to giving more formal speeches later in the school year.

Practicing Oral Presentation Skills

Informal speaking activities conducted early in the semester can help students develop confidence for longer speeches in class. You can see how well they are moving along meeting the curriculum standards for your course that ask students to demonstrate how well they can "present information, findings, and supporting evidence such that listeners can follow the line of reasoning."[3]

You can give holistic grades as you evaluate your teaching so far. This can be a *win-win-win* situation and speed you along your school year journey without missing the views along the way. Students hear about books they may decide to read and you get to measure what they know and are able to do with the lessons you have taught, modeled, and given them time to practice.

CONCLUSION

The key to introducing narrative theory is to use examples and illustrations from stories that engage students and keep them reading, viewing, listening, and sharing stories. Use stories from the class text along with downloadable media files, especially short video clips. Keep in mind this introduction or review of literary terms is designed to ensure that your students have the vocabulary with which to talk and write about the way fiction, prose, and poetry are shaped.

The short-term goal is to have a common word base and academic concepts of the grammar of fiction and a concrete understanding of these elements of literature. The longer-term goal is to prepare your middle school students with knowledge and skills that can serve them well in high school and later, when they participate in neighborhood book discussion groups as adults. Right?

NOTES

1. Sybylla Y. Hendrix, "Why Our Students Study Literature." Gustavus Adolphus College. http://gustavus.edu/academics/english/whystudyliterature.php (accessed April 3, 2012).

2. "English Language Arts Standards » Anchor Standards » College and Career Readiness Anchor Standards for Language." Common Core State Standards Initiative. 2011. http://www.corestandards.org/ELA-Literacy/ (accessed July 4, 2018).

3. English Language Arts Standards. Anchor Standards.

Chapter 3

Crossing into Novel Territory: Reading Longer Fiction

In Robert Newton Peck's award-winning young adult novel, *A Day No Pigs Would Die*, a young boy queries his father:

> "Fences are funny, aren't they, Papa?"
>
> "How so?"
>
> "Well, you be friends with Mr. Tanner. Neighbors and all. But we keep this fence up like it was war. I guess that humans are the only things on earth that take everything they own and fence it off." . . .
>
> "I never looked at it that way."
>
> "Time you did."[1]

In this twentieth-century novel, father and son discuss how human beings create "fences," including physical and social walls between ethnic groups, generations, and individuals. It is likely that your students are noticing such fences and are beginning to learn about those who live across the fences in their own lives. They see in the media issues related to gender, race, ethnicity, language, social class, disability, age, and religion.

Peck's moving novel offers a peek into the world of a twelve-year-old boy who wonders about the real value of socially constructed fences, some of which he wants to tear down, others he comes to understand, if not accept. This chapter offers ideas for teaching this novel by Peck in ways that you can adapt to a full-length, age-appropriate work of fiction in the course you teach.

For some students, peeking across the fence into the adult world can be like a trip off to a planet where you can view, venture into, and explore new territories. This boy's father, Vermont farmer Haven Peck, makes ends meet in the late 1920s by slaughtering pigs for others to eat. Why does the elder Peck earn a living that way? Do people really have to kill and eat pigs? Peck's son has to come to terms with adult reality.

Modern writings like Peck's help readers discover other contemporary people and cultures. It can be frightening and confusing for adolescents to traverse childhood fences. But reading about life beyond one's fences can also be fun, engaging, and relevant to students' lives.

Through such reading, students get to explore key ideas that can help meet course curriculum standards in areas like craft and structure as well as the ways authors of long works use some of the same literary devices as those who write short stories. Sometimes the apparent distance between reality and fantasy makes the latter a safe way to discuss tough issues in diverse classroom settings. So, feel free to include fantasy and science fiction on your reading lists.

As an educator, you have the honor of and responsibility for guiding students across fences into stories about other persons and places, helping your learners to engage various literary forms and themes depicting other cultures. You can inspire students to interpret, understand, and respond critically to modern literature in the context of their own multimedia lives as they cross literary fences into novel territory.

This chapter explains how you can teach modern literature by delving with your students into, through, and beyond a work of fiction. Here are strategies described by the California Reading and Literacy Project.

MOVING INTO, THROUGH, AND BEYOND A BOOK

Get into the book by

- encouraging students to make initial predictions;
- providing background information; and
- identifying text-related vocabulary.

Work through the book by

- reading aloud to the students;
- having students read aloud and silently during class;
- challenging students through active reading;
- guiding students to write about the work;
- connecting the book to students' lives; and
- fostering class discussion with student- and teacher-generated questions.

Move beyond the book by

- assessing student comprehension with performance and/or product options;

- assigning projects and essays;
- getting students involved in research about the book and its culture(s); and
- inspiring students to read more.

As you read further in this chapter, you can add to your suitcase preparing yourself to teach ways that contemporary authors employ the essential elements of fiction. Here are concrete examples from Peck's novel to demonstrate how you can reach and revive readers with skills and literacies to flourish in today's multicultural, multimedia societies.

PREPLANNING THE UNIT

To ease your anxiety, if you are teaching a book for the first time, estimate how much class time you need to spend on the book. Consider

- your school's homework guidelines and curricular goals;
- the language arts standards of your course; and
- the interests, skills, and needs of your students, perhaps as reported by teachers who have had the students in English the previous year.

Estimate how many pages of fiction your students can handle per day. Then plan a realistic reading schedule before launching the unit.

Building Background

Depending on the book you are teaching, you may find it useful to bring in picture books to supplement your lessons. For example, to prepare for or to expand the conversation about fences and society, bring in and share *Talking Walls* written by Margy Burns Knight and illustrated by Anne Sibley O'Brien. Use it to launch discussions about figurative walls and fences used to separate and/or protect. Other picture books provide background information about people, places, and events that help students better understand the fictional works you may choose to explore.

Deciding What Vocabulary

Vocabulary study is a topic to consider pedagogically before and during students' reading. For example, if you did not grow up on a farm, you may lack experience of the smells and sounds mentioned in Peck's novel set in rural Vermont. The same may be true for your students and the text you are teaching.

Whichever modern book you use for class, be sure to introduce the students to the cultural language of the text; identify vocabulary students might not know and determine how best to provide definitions or elicit definitions from them. It is perfectly fine to give students definitions of words unique to the book. Showing pictures illustrating vocabulary is particularly helpful for English language learners.

Vocabulary they need to add to their speaking and writing vocabulary can be handled differently. Consider: What words do students need to know to read the opening chapters of this book and other books set for this course to understand general reading as adults?

Encourage students to create their own lists of new words as they read. Write in their journals and indicate the page number for each word or phrase. Then you can pull twenty or twenty-five words common to their lists, explore definitions together, and discuss them as they relate to the book. You can also ask the students to check print or digital dictionaries and then write their own one-sentence definitions that fit the context of their reading. It is not useful to have students learn all the definitions of every vocabulary word on the list. Focus instead on the word meanings that help them understand this particular piece of literature.

RECORD IT! VIDEO JOURNALING

If students are already interested and motivated, you might want to allow groups of two or three students to make video recordings based on their

Talking about a topic is not the same as *teaching*

written journals. You can ask them to write one journal entry as a group, collaborating on the content, but then delegating responsibilities for: (1) final drafting for reading on camera, (2) operating the camera, and (3) editing out any retakes. Using most digital cameras, they can save and upload it to your school computer server. In some cases, you might allow them to post their video journals to a school server or websites like YouTube, but only after making sure that they will not identify themselves personally on the recordings or in the accompanying text captions. The ideal length for these video journal entries is about forty-five to sixty seconds. Students should include copies of the video script outlines in their journals.

For assessment, remind your budding video producers that video journals should display neatness—clear images, good visual grammar—editing for pacing that enables the viewer-listener to follow along, and correct pronunciation and spelling in written information.

COVERING IS NOT THE SAME AS TEACHING

Until students can understand and engage a text, you are not ready to go on to the next piece of literature. Even with a modern text, moving too quickly leads to superficial student understandings. On the other hand, moving too slowly misses opportunities for greater textual engagement. So, determine students' critical abilities, monitor their progress, and make appropriate scheduling and pedagogical adjustments as you go.

You can help them read more deeply, critically, and efficiently as you remind them of, and teach them, a range of strategies to increase their reading comprehension. Depending on where they attended school before, your students may be familiar with some of these ideas. But because adolescents seem to have a more positive attitude toward more recently written literature, it often is better to teach and add these approaches to reading literature while working with a modern book rather than with a more challenging classic novel or complex poetry. Reviewing what has been taught is an efficient use of time, especially if you present the same information in new ways.

GETTING INTO THE BOOK

A great place to begin a unit on the novel is by having students create a "novels" section in their written journals or a new folder on the digital one, and then create subsections for the novels that you assign throughout the year. Their journal is a personal place for them to write their own reading summaries, responses, reflections, vocabulary study, diagrams, and drawings along with questions like those mentioned in Chapter Two on teaching the short story.

Playing Online Audio and Video Files

If quality readings of the book's opening are available online, select and play excerpts from them in class. YouTube and other video-posting websites sometimes include acceptable fan readings. Avoid performance video clips that might frame the book visually for students before they have developed their own mental pictures of characters and settings. Chances are you have one or two tech-savvy students who can find recordings, download them, and bring them to you for previewing before playing them for their peers. Remember, what is done in your class reflects you.

Begin lessons on journaling with a random walk through the book as described in Chapter Two, or with open questions to familiarize your students with this longer form of fiction. Questions might include:

- Do you recall a book that grabbed you from the first sentence? How would you define a "novel"?
- Other than length, how do you think a full-length book is different from a short story or a movie?
- Based on the title of this book, how do you think it relates to an essential question or theme we have been talking about so far this year? Some departments suggest essential questions for teachers to consider for a quarter, semester, or full school year.

In other settings, teachers choose broad questions from the myriad online sources that suggest questions like:

- What is the relationship between decisions and consequences?
- What allows some individuals to take a stand against prejudice/oppression while others choose to participate in it?
- How are people transformed through their relationships with others?

Try to create an open, exciting experience for students while monitoring responses to questions that make your readers feel ill at ease. Resist commenting on their responses, even with facial expressions. Encourage honesty; insist on courtesy. Demonstrate what you teach.

Your opening attitude sets the tone for the class. If they know that you enjoy fiction, they are more likely to read it expectantly. However, there is no reason to try to gin up false enthusiasm for a literary work you do not like. Even if you do not prefer reading fiction, you can share your enthusiasm for learning about something new. Of course, you want to allot time for them to read books they choose themselves. So, continue to reward but not penalize students who cannot do much independent reading. You know your school setting. Develop goals and help students develop skill and opportunity to reach them.

Few students take pleasure in a book if they do not understand the cultural context, time period, unusual references, and difficult vocabulary. So, before you assign them to read too far in the book, spark their critical interest in the story and give them some helpful tools to begin enjoying and discussing the text right away.

Inspire desire to explore new texts

Sparking Critical Interest in the Story

You can ignite interest in the book and elicit visual interpretation by having students do something as simple as examining the cover art of a paperback or the drawing included with the text in your class anthology. Give the students two or three minutes to examine that art and print, individually or in small groups. Then ask them to predict and answer the following kinds of questions in their journals:

- Based on the graphic art, what do you imagine this book is about? (If there is a synopsis on the cover or first page, you might need to modify this question.)
- What have you already heard about this book—and does that word-of-mouth fit with your view of the artwork?
- What do you know about the topic/setting of the book? For example, for A *Day No Pigs Would Die*, what do you know about raising pigs, the state of Vermont, or about the origin of baseball?

No cover illustration? Check online bookstores or the publisher's website to see if you can find cover images for past paperback or hardcover editions. Even without a cover image, it's worth discussing the book design graphics. In this case, try asking: (1) Why do you think the publishers chose certain fonts, font sizes, colors, or word placements?; (2) What is the name of the font(s)?; (3) Why may there be no graphics—photos, drawings, and so on?; (4) What do the comments on the book cover or reviewer comments make you think about this book?; and (5) Where else do you hear or read comments about the arts (e.g., movie trailers and newspaper or web ads for movies)?

These metatextual strategies—ways of talking about how texts communicate—create curiosity about the book. They also encourage the groups of students to own their learning, since they can clearly learn from one another as well as from you. Students soon discover that it is educationally good to formulate and express opinions, reasonable interpretations, and evaluations of texts. Finally, students who think only classic writing should be analyzed soon learn that modern texts can be examined as well as enjoyed—and that criticism can lead to greater enjoyment. In this case, criticism should not be limited to simple statements of opinions. Encourage students to expand their opinion statements with specific reasons. Remember, students do not have to like a literary work in order to appreciate it. See the "Nine Yardsticks of Value" prompts in chapter 1.

Locate and display images of the time period and/or part of the country to create intrigue. Consider bringing in items to suggest characters or events ahead of time, and just setting them up in the classroom until needed.

Sometimes a short poem on one of the topics in the books is just the thing to jump-start a book. Occasionally projecting a photograph or piece of artwork will suffice.

Using Student-Produced PowerPoints to Facilitate Early Discussion

As you begin discussion with students, write on the board one- or two-word responses of their initial thoughts and feelings about the book. Then encourage interested students to compose simple PowerPoint slide(s) that contain one of these short summaries using font and background colors designed to match the meaning of the summary. Students can add relevant highlighting or other features that help them explain their view of the book.

Fonts and colors can "speak" to readers even though these visual images are not as literarily precise as "word language." This kind of assignment teaches media grammar, too. Check out online sites to help familiarize yourself with media grammar if this is a new concept for you. A student interested in drama might want to speak the word(s) interpretively as a looping soundtrack for each image.

Your tech-savvy students may be interested in experimenting with a version of the Pecha Kucha format for this preliminary activity or as a final project. Simply put, this means creating twenty slides set to advance every twenty seconds as a speaker narrates. You may decide to create and model this format to introduce the modern novel to supplement your instruction for a piece of literature and then make this format an optional student assignment later in the school year.

Finally, students doing multislide presentations (one word or phrase per slide) can add a sound track that relates to the novel's subject or characters. Search the topic "pig lyrics." Students may wish to create one for Peck's novel. PowerPoint's player function creates a short "motion picture" that sets a pre-reading benchmark for later review. If students enjoy seeing the PowerPoint in class, consider showing it again at the end of the unit to discuss initial versus later impressions of the novel. It is efficient to show before semester exams, too.

Caution: Try creating these kinds of slides yourself to see what skills and time are needed to complete them. You may find the depth of thinking and reflecting required are worth the time you allot for such alternative ways to look at and depict various genres of literature.

Applying Something Old to Something New

How about adapting one of those KWL charts that students probably used in elementary school? This graphic organizer that asks students what they

KNOW, WANT to learn, and have LEARNED can be useful in classes with older students, too. Working with the familiar makes the unfamiliar less daunting. It's like seeing a McDonald's sign in the middle of the desert.

What do students know about Vermont (or the setting of your book), about the Shakers (or a social, regional, racial group in your book), about the origins of baseball (or a cultural event in your book), about this historical period, and so on? What do they hope to discover as they read? Save these charts for later in the unit. An opening class activity during the weeks that you are reading the book could be to spend a few minutes filling in the "L" column or adding to the "W" column. If the book does not reveal answers to these questions, they could be the basis of a final project or performance in which students conduct brief research and then share in a written or artistic way what they learn.

Organizing Quotations

Photocopy a randomized list of the quotations from the book you plan to teach. (Leave off the page numbers.)

Ask the students to put the quotations in an order that makes sense to them.

Meet in pairs to compare the order. (Order is unimportant at this point. Thinking is.)

Then talk briefly about what they think the book is about. What inferences can they make based simply on these quotations? (This is a good way to highlight the sentence structure the author uses, too.)

Letting Authors Speak for Themselves

While it is important to provide some background for the book, initially it is good to let the text speak for itself. Give the students only the information that they need to understand the beginning of the story. Then, as the story unfolds, supply additional information. Even if you have had to do a lot of research yourself to prepare to teach an unfamiliar book, remember not to inundate the students with all of your newfound knowledge—TMI (too much information), which can overshadow, even bury the book. On a trip, it would be like touring five different museums on the same day! Just too much to appreciate the craftsmanship of those whose work is on display.

A host of textbooks, websites, academic books, and colleagues can help inform your own understanding of the text, but during class, resist dumping all this newfound knowledge on the students. First, focus on the basic aspects of the time and place that students need to know to figure out the plot, setting, and characters in the novel. In carefully selected, engaging books of fiction and nonfiction, the authors can speak for themselves.

WORKING THROUGH THE BOOK

Reading to Students

Adolescents, like many adults, enjoy hearing good readers. Think about how often you and your peers purchase, borrow audio books, or attend events where authors read from their books. So, it is not surprising that an appealing way to begin teaching a book is to read portions aloud to your students. This gives unengaged readers a chance to learn by listening and following along. It supports English language learners, because it helps them confirm the sound of the language to the printed words.

Since some international students' first language uses a non-English-style alphabet, they might need practice associating sounds with the written English letters as they work to improve their basic reading literacy. Hearing the words as they watch the text is another way to increase this association and expand their comprehension.

Try connecting early on with students' multiple intelligences by assigning different activities for them to do while listening in class. Some might sketch in their journals what is happening in the story, mold with clay, or jot notes in a chart with story events. Many multitasking students prefer to listen to music while studying. Since there is no "right" way to read, as long as students are keeping up and comprehending the text, engage non-aural learners

Listening to a book is another way to experience the writer's words

with appropriate ways to formulate and express textual interpretations. Consider playing instrumental music during silent reading time. Music played in a rhythm that matches the beat of the heart at rest calms listeners and helps them to focus.

Reading Silently

Although reading aloud to students is good pedagogy, students also need to be able to learn by reading silently. You can help students stay on schedule by providing in-class reading periods. Doing so eliminates the frustration for students unable to participate in class discussions simply because they are behind on reading. Consider having a prompt or question on the board before students arrive. Then ask them to use the first five to seven minutes of class to peruse their reading to find text evidence to support their answer or just to catch up on the reading. Walk around the room and peek at what they are writing.

As they write, circulate among them while taking attendance but also stopping near individuals, adding to your own notes indications of student engagement in the task. Journaling in this simple writing activity focuses students on the day's topic while you complete record-keeping.

Observing their responses and watching them read can also help you identify students who may be experiencing difficulties. Pay attention to how long

Intentional observation is effective formative assessment

it takes individuals to complete a page of reading. If you have concerns, but not the expertise, to address them yourself, seek the assistance of a reading specialist or the advice of the department chair or a colleague.

Students Reading to the Class and in Pairs or Groups

Occasionally, give students the chance to read aloud with the whole class, in small groups or to a partner. Students who especially dislike reading aloud may need to practice in a nonthreatening setting. You can invite such students to read aloud short passages of their choosing just to you; you can track their progress and encourage them personally. Remind students that public speaking skills are important for most careers and reading aloud can help them practice their articulation—clear pronunciation of words. Students work harder at it if they know that reading aloud is a significant step toward career success. For English language learners with access to recent technology, encourage them to read aloud on a talk-to-text program to confirm their pronunciation improvements.

Of course, you have the hams, too, who just love to play parts from the book. The dialogue in the text provides exceptional ways for students to gain insight into the personalities of the characters in the book. Encourage dramatic oral reading, but be fair and have students take turns reading aloud the most popular characters. Play the narrator if you want to ensure that the reading stays on track.

READING ACTIVELY

It is essential for students' future education that they become critical readers. Students know that people read books for fun, but they might not realize that adults also read fiction and nonfiction simply to enrich their lives. In short, students who read widely and attentively deepen their understanding of different cultures as well as the human condition. Students benefit when they learn that active reading requires careful attention to the text, regardless of the medium—print or electronic, aural or visual. In travel, it's like learning to read the road signs, those with words and those with universal symbols. It helps you get where you're going without getting lost, too many times.

One essential skill in active reading is recognizing how subparts of a larger text relate to one another. These text structures, sometimes called "rhetorical structures," include descriptive, sequential, enumerative, cause-effect, problem/solution, and compare/contrast relationships within a text.

Assuming Personae in Fiction and Biographical Writing

Once they have "met" the main characters, ask your students to sign up to keep a journal from their chosen or assigned character's perspective and write two or three sentence entries for each section of the assigned reading. Allot in-class time for small group meetings of those writing from the same character's point of view. Mix it up some days and construct groups with different characters meeting together to talk for a few moments about the way their character is addressing the problems in the book. Is he or she:

- making wise or foolish choices?
- assisting or thwarting the protagonist?
- alike or different from someone the student knows?

If your learners have enjoyed this personae perspective, you could follow up their reading of the book with an assignment that asks them to connect their person with current events and answer questions like: "What would your chosen character have to say about something in the news today? What issues would interest them? What television shows or movies would he or she like?"

When students read fiction, they enter into a story created by the author. They let the author transport them into a projected, imaginary "world." To accomplish this world-projecting storytelling, the author structures:

- relationships among characters,
- characters' motivation, and
- causal relationships between characters' thoughts and actions.

Because of these author-created structures—along with readers' own real-life relationships—students begin to predict certain things to occur in the story. As they learn more about the structure of these longer works, students' expectations rise in similar ways.

Tracking Character Development

Students wonder why characters think and act in certain ways. As they read, they speculate about why particular events lead to other events—like the age-old conundrums about why bad things happen to good people. Students begin mentally asking the same kinds of questions about fiction that they ask about life, and language arts teachers can help the learners develop strategies to help comprehend, interpret, and evaluate their reading. As they gain skills to identify and examine the impact of intra-text structures in their own reading, students engage the story or article as if conversing with the author and the characters.

Continue to encourage students to write in their journals the questions that arise when reading.

Offering Prompts for Journal Writing

So how do students move from the book itself toward a more critical dialogue with it? The conversation has to start somewhere, but some of your students will not have practiced taking notes when they see a movie, play a YouTube video, listen to an audio book, or read fiction. Therefore, a reader-response journal can effectively initiate their personal dialogue with a text.

In this type of journal, students

- transcribe or copy important passages,
- record their own questions about the text,
- note what they enjoy in the text, and
- indicate important material for the later study.

Students can also journal in their textbooks with sticky notes so they do not have to recopy the text sections in their journals. Some e-books have features for inserting annotations, too. Then they can copy those thoughts into their separate journal notebook, save or copy into their digital journals while keeping the sticky notes or electronic notations for quick reference in their books.

You might even suggest that students use different color techniques to code story elements or text structure and log their reactions, especially their questions. Propose that students use a specific color to note passages that strike them as potentially effective video or audio scenes for later recording. Here, also, is a place to use emojis to record graphic responses to reading. See Box 3.1 for ideas to mark text.

Invite students to visualize what is going on in the book based on the author's direct and indirect statements. Drawing maps and pictures in their journals helps some students hold on to those visualizations. Some students working online may find themselves doing searches to view items or places mentioned in their reading. Encourage such exploration; it enriches comprehension and expands the overall reading experience, especially when they share their drawings with peers.

> **BOX 3.0 SYMBOLS FOR MARKING TEXT OR MAKING JOURNAL NOTES**
>
> Consider using text-marking symbols to remind students of the kinds of things that they should be noting and responding to in the text. Here are some basic text-engaging symbols:
>
> ☺ = I understand; I knew that.
>
> ! = Wow! I didn't know that!
>
> *** = This is important. I should remember this.
>
> ▢ = New character is introduced (write name and words that identify the character, such as "George, 10 years old").
>
> → = Great visual image—I can picture it in my mind.
>
> ? = I don't understand. Ask about this.

HIGHLIGHTING ACADEMIC VOCABULARY

What about terms in the text that the students should be adding to their own speaking and writing vocabulary? What about words used in the book that also appear in reading and conversations your students have in other classes? And what about general academic vocabulary used primarily in school? You can help students learn the meanings of, and connections among, words by identifying such academic words on their vocabulary list and asking students themselves to find the definitions in print or online dictionaries. You do not have to do everything.

Invite students to list the words with definitions alphabetically on a class website or post comparative definitions on a class online document. The shared document itself then serves as a kind of study sheet students can print out or download to their own computers. The words that are specific to the text, though, are those for which you can provide definitions.

Like many veteran teachers, you may find it productive to maintain a word wall to which you add new words throughout the school year. Seeing is believing. As students view the wall daily, they catch on that it is important to learn and use the words. On a trip, it's like seeing the same advertisement on road signs. Soon you remember them and may even decide to visit the site or purchase the product. The same can happen with your students. What they see, they remember; what they remember, they are likely to use.

Reinforce the importance of students using new vocabulary words in their prose by offering small amounts of extra credit for incorporating the terms in writing for other classes. Sure, other teachers may question the ways that your students use the words. But once the students explain that they are trying to expand their vocabulary, your colleagues are likely to support the students' work even if the vocabulary sticks out as unexpectedly as an elephant in a flock of sheep. Challenge your students to use their vocabulary regularly even if they are teased for their increased sophistication and even if they earn the maximum of ten points per quarter!

Dividing the Labor Can Multiply the Results

Since most students love to talk anyway, create small groups who will be responsible for just a few of the words on the list. For example, if your list has twenty words, have five groups who each are responsible for showing the meaning of four words. In addition to the traditional information usually required in vocabulary study, add photos that can be uploaded into a computer program and then shared on a class wiki or projected in a digital presentation.

Calling on Cell Phones for Vocabulary Study: A Mini-Assignment

1. Locate the assigned word in the literature being studied.
2. Determine how it is used (what part of speech) in the context of the literary work.
3. Look up the word in a good dictionary that includes more than synonyms.
4. Locate or photograph images to help classmates understand the meaning of each assigned word. The image should reflect the literal and/or figurative meaning—one that will serve as a mnemonic for the word.
5. Create and photograph original art work, use computer graphics, stage a scene with toys, or have classmates pose for a scene.
6. Consider color, font, image, or music to portray the meaning of the word as used in the context of the literary work being studied.
7. Then, as a group, create one- to two-minute slide or video presentation that reflects what the group has learned about the words, including original sentences using the words and synonyms, antonyms, and/or appositives to help clarify the meaning.

This assignment utilizes the range of skills of a typical group of students who represent the multiple intelligences; it has active and passive tasks that appeal to students of both genders and with varying levels of English language proficiency.

The assignment is sure to be a success if you

- design the lessons carefully to last three to five days;
- have written instructions to supplement the oral ones;
- demonstrate a sample product with the class helping you gather information on one vocabulary word;
- allot ten to fifteen minutes of class time during the final fifteen minutes of class the first week that literature is being studied; and
- set a digital timer each day to reserve the closing fifteen minutes for small group work and five minutes for clearing up and closing the lesson for the day.

During these two weeks, present your start of class lessons, as usual, orienting students to the literary work: historical background and personal information about the author, reminding them of the language of literature they already know. Then use the remainder of class that first week for this kind of vocabulary work.

It's worth the in-class time for such group work and language study. It can be an opportunity to do no-stress formative assessments of your students that will help you adjust your instruction as you plan for further lessons. It gives students time to do what they do best—work together and learn from one another while exploring and applying skills that lead to meeting a range of language arts standards.

DEVELOPING DIVERSE PERSONAL CONNECTIONS TO CONTEMPORARY NOVELS

The key is helping students to recognize three things. First, a novelist's imaginative story is usually a mirror for some people even if it is not a mirror for others, such as your students.

Second, students can discover that other people's mirrors can serve as windows for getting to know those who are different from themselves. Windows become venues for self-understanding as students begin to see similarities among those they read about and those with whom they live.

Third, reading about others enables students to see what human beings have in common, across their cultural fences. Novels express not only cultural particularities of time and place, but also common aspects of the human condition, such as fear and loneliness, joy and delight, agreement and disagreement. For instance, adolescents in every culture eventually come of age; the process is universal even though it takes different cultural forms. Metaphorical windows can help students to understand simultaneously themselves, their communities, other persons, and other communities.

Relating through Personal Connections

As mentioned earlier, textual literacy includes the ability to relate critically the fictional worlds to one's own life. These reader-to-self, reader-to-world, or reader-to-text relationships can work in multiple ways. Yes, as mirrors and windows, but sometimes also sliding glass doors that do both—reflect and provide a way in or out.

As a mirror, novels reflect familiar characters, settings, and situations. As a window, novels introduce students to unfamiliar people, places, and circumstances—including cultures, ethnicities, races, and geographies. As often as you can, select books that help to expand your students understanding of themselves and of others, to see across and through fences into novel territory. Include options to read nonfiction, like biographies and autobiographies and see your skeptical readers bloom into eager ones.

Encourage conversation, but guide it so it does not become denigrating or disrespectful of what is different or simply unfamiliar. Choosing culturally relevant books and articles means more than selecting writing by and about the ethnicities represented in your school or classroom. It also means

Encourage students to keep notes as they read

literature that introduces and expands your students' experience to those groups not represented there in your school community.

Honoring Student Privacy

Ask students to journal about their personal connections with the world of the book; such journaling promotes discussion because students articulate in writing thoughts they can then paraphrase out loud. Just remember that some students are reticent about reading or discussing their reflections with the entire class. Respect their privacy and you can gain their trust and motivate them to read deeply and write honestly.

Consider giving students the option in class of folding down the page in their written journals if they do not want you to read their reflections. If you provide that option, keep your promise but do inform them. If anything they write and leave open for you to read makes you believe they are in danger to themselves or others, you are bound by law to report it to authorities.

Also warn students about posting personal information online, since privacy is a major issue in the information age. One of the reasons that social networking websites such as Facebook are so popular is that students think they regulate who they allow to access their postings by approving who their "friends" are—those who can access their website. But no public site is totally secure, and what is posted today as a lark may be embarrassing or even dangerous tomorrow.

Privacy and tact are important literary issues; openness and honesty are essential to building trust in the classroom. So, write in your own journal frequently, right along with your students. Doing so not only models this kind of writing but also reminds you of what it is like to reveal text-to-self connections with others.

Share with your students some of the experiences you have had with your parents, siblings, and friends—and also admit that there are some experiences you would, and they should, not write about online. If you respect students' privacy, they are more likely to share their journals with you—and they learn that responding to readings should be an ethical as well as an academic practice. In other words, invite rather than insist that they share or show what they write to others.

INSPIRING CLASS DISCUSSION

English teachers often approach the study of a book or article by giving students a list of discussion questions. This can effectively ease students into the

Allot time to search for images of vocabulary words

reading and demonstrate the types of questions and ideas that they should be considering. But you foster better, more engaging discussions if you encourage students to come up with their own thoughtful, life-connected, and text-connected questions.

Regardless of how you settle on the questions, try a variety of discussion group formats—pairs, small groups, and the entire class. Some students are more inclined to read their journal entries and discuss personal responses to the text if they are in smaller groups. Still, many like to push the envelope, test the boundaries, and interject topics that are on the edge—just for fun or attention—so it is important to circulate among them as they read and talk about their writing.

If a student offers an inappropriate remark, then a moment's eye contact, subtle head shake, or quiet admonition from you should be enough to refocus the discussion. As on a road trip, when the sheriff is spotted, drivers adjust their driving behavior—and so do your students; when you are nearby, they are reminded of the rules of the road as they pertain to the class.

Interspersing Literature Circles

Think about setting up literature circles for a few chapters in the book your class is studying together. For this approach to reading and discussing literature, you create small groups of five or six students and assign or let them draw role names or numbers to perform certain tasks. These responsibilities may include

- making connections between what the class has already read and the book they currently are reading;
- pointing out ways words on the vocabulary list are being used;
- selecting a particularly interesting, humorous, or thought-provoking passage to read aloud to the members of the group;
- drawing a picture of a scene that is crucial to the plot or understanding of a character;
- bringing in an appropriate prop that illustrates an incident or symbolizes a character; and/or
- keeping time to assure that the group completes the tasks in the allotted time.

The tasks can vary depending on the book you have chosen. See figure 1.1 in chapter 1 for a way to model, and then schedule literature circles.

Adapting Think, Pair, Share Strategies

Have students work independently to think about a prompt, then pair up and talk with a partner before one or both of them share or report out to the whole class. This is an effective way to begin discussions about difficult passages or controversial topics, especially with shy students or those who tend to leap over into the driver's seat if not kept in their seat belts. Consider adding another layer to this familiar strategy and recommend that students find support for their responses in the text you may be having them read that day.

As the students are writing their answers, you could circulate among them, looking over their shoulders seeing who goes directly to a likely place in the text to find the answer. Don't be surprised if they go to an unexpected section and still come up with a valid response. When you notice that the majority of the students have something written, you could call on the ones who have different, but valid, maybe even opposing answers. Then ask the class who agrees that Student A's answer seems logical and who thinks Student B's answer seems stronger. You could follow up asking students to find additional evidence from the text that supports A or B.

Of course, modeling first and providing answer stems can help students get started. For example, in Gary Schmidt's *Wednesday Wars* "I believe Mrs. Baker is . . . because . . . and this section on page . . . supports my observation." Or, "Character A is a jerk because . . . and when you look at page . . . you'll see that I'm right." Or, "The passage on page . . . suggests the principal is prejudiced . . . because of the way the author uses negative images," or whatever.

Even though you may decide to conduct whole class discussions, you still could incorporate some of the literature circle roles. If the majority of your students are reliable about completing homework, once you introduce the roles, invite students to sign up for the role they would like to play for the next LIT CIRCLE–type discussion. Then assign for homework their gathering information to fill that role during the next class meeting.

The next day you could have the students playing the same roles meet to compare answers during the first ten minutes of class, then invite them as a panel to present their answers to the class. Or, after the small group meeting, you could reconfigure the class so that each group includes at least one person fulfilling each role and have them "teach" that group what they learned.

You may know this organizational pattern as jig-saw grouping. Each of these strategies increases student confidence about speaking out loud among their peers and deepens their understanding of the text. Your English language learners may even flourish in these settings.

WRITING ABOUT A BOOK IN-CLASS

Develop three questions about the recent reading, then ask students to answer one using specific references and selected quotations from a specified section. For example, have them refer to five of the seven chapters read so far and incorporate the illustrative facts and words smoothly into the text of their essay writing. Encourage answering the question in their thesis statement as part of their introduction paragraph, then writing two or three body paragraphs that make a hearty P.I.E. with lots of rich, meaty filling, concluding with a summary or reflection on what they have written in the body paragraphs.

P = Point—state your point or position in response to the prompt
I = Illustrate—support your point with two or three direct references to the story. One of these can be a short quotation. "For example . . ." (Give the page number in parenthesis following the reference or quotation.)
E = Explain—the connection between your illustrations and your point. "This shows . . ."

One of the themes in *A Day No Pigs Would Die* is that something may die in order for something else to live. When searching the novel, students find these examples: a cow nearly dies birthing the twin calves; a crow gobbles a frog; and the narrator's family eats animals they slaughter for food. Ultimately, Rob, the main character, suffers the death of his father and has to assist his mother with farm tasks, including killing his own pet pig so the family can have food to eat. A few students become so enamored of Rob's

Meaty P.I.E. paragraphs demonstrate deep reading and good writing

pet, Piggy, that they convert and become vegans—at least while studying the novel. Of course, even as vegans they consume formerly living things. All life depends on other life.

TESTING THOUGHTS ON THEME

While studying a book, students can examine further concepts of theme—the overall message(s) of a text, or what the text is trying to say about a topic. The concept of literature itself is sometimes defined by a work's universal themes about human nature and the human condition as well as by its aesthetic qualities. Themes, though, generally are statements about topics, not just the topics themselves; themes require a verb to indicate the author's viewpoint. "Life is grand" is a theme; "Life" is a subject, but not a theme. "Fences make good neighbors" is a theme; "fences" is simply a topic.

Your students may have been introduced to this kind of thinking about literature in elementary school and used the SWBST approach. There they would fill in a graphic organizer in which they record what Somebody Wanted, But, So and Then, to reflect the main characters, the conflict, the attempts to solve it, and then the resolution. Using this SWBST chart may be a good place to start and then move on to sentence statements about the book.

After you explain to students the concept of universal theme, let them try to discern what may or may not be a universal theme expressed through the novel you are studying together. Invite students to experiment with theme statements in their own reading and journaling. What is the story saying to them?

Also, ask them to test or verify their ideas about themes with specific, supporting examples from the beginning, middle, and the end of the novel. Students soon notice that most books have at least two or three overarching ideas that can be summarized in thematic statements that capture most individual responses to the text. In the biography or autobiography, what experiences are described that reflect what is true about people in general?

GRADING STUDENT RESPONSES TO A BOOK

Encourage formal and informal student responses to the book. Since informal writing is more personal, students should earn full credit just for demonstrating that they have read the selected material and responded responsibly to the prompt. Formal writing, on the other hand, calls for more precise literary analysis and is graded for form and accuracy as well as content. Consider the following samples from student journals:

Student #1 journal essay was a "Five W's and H Summary" (the journalistic who, what, where, why, when, and how) based on seven to ten verbs that describe the plot. She wrote this entry after two months of studying the elements of fiction and reading a number of short stories for which students were writing this kind of summary.

Student Journal Entry #1

Robert cut school because he was made fun of. He found a cow who was in labor and having a calf. He is in Vermont, and 12 years old. He desperately tries to help the cow, because she is in pain and when the cow chokes, he reaches down her throat and pulls out the "goiter." She bites his arm and pulls him all around. His arm was gnawed and flesh was missing. He gets stitches and after being in bed for about a week, he goes to help his pa. Their neighbor that owns the cow thanks Robert for helping her, and given him a pig! Robert is excited. His dad informs him of the care it takes to own a pig. Then they talk some more.

About a week after beginning a book, once students have closely read and discussed the exposition, your students should be ready to write personal responses, normally by answering "what" and "why" questions. Reading their personal responses helps you learn which parts of the story interest students as well as whether they are missing important details that would then need to be addressed in class. You also learn more about the students as people—which can help with planning subsequent lessons to better meet learners' academic needs and accommodate their varied interests.

To prepare students to write analytically, ask them to write journal entries in which they focus their attention on the elements of fiction or specific literary devices. Another student chose to write about symbols and similes. She understood the former but not the latter device. Her incomplete Journal Entry #2 did not include an explanation of why each of her quotations is a symbol or a simile. Thankfully, seeing her entry before the test revealed that she needed help in identifying the ways that authors use symbols and similes. After she and others had reviews in class, this student handled these kinds of questions well on the test.

Student Journal Entry #2

Peck uses symbols as similes. On page number 104, it says, "And during fair week, I guest it's like a big brass band that can't stop playing." Another time he uses a symbol is still on page 104. It says, "Just like a mouth I know that's got blackberry all over it. These are both symbols in the book.

A third student rambled in "Journal Entry #3." But his entry revealed which incidents caught his attention and which ones needed clarification. Sometimes students ask questions in class; other times questions arise only in students' writing.

Student Journal Entry #3

One of the things about this book is that it will start out with a conflict, then tell why that conflict arose. For instance, in the end of this section of the . . . [sic]. There is a man that goes and digs up his daughter from her grave. I didn't really understand the whole conflict of why he couldn't dig her up. Oh, also we now have proof that Robert is a Shaker because he goes to the meetings. I'm amazed that a pig would get to be as big as twelve year old boys. Because unless they get any bigger than that I probably wouldn't believe it was unless I saw it.

ASSIGNING PROJECTS AND ESSAYS

As you do when planning each assignment, determine what you need to know about student understanding and design product or performance assessments through which students can demonstrate that knowledge.

Differentiating Assessments

Plan a wide variety of projects for assessing students via multiple intelligences. For example, let a musically inclined student write a song about the book or choose songs that appropriately reflect certain characters. Let an aspiring filmmaker produce a scene of an incident from the book. Design assessments to measure what you need to know.

In other words, every test does not have to be only writing; instead, include requirements for written explanations for choices made about components of products or performances students submit to show what they know. Ask them to tell, using specific references or quotations from the text, why they chose specific images, movements, music, or details.

Identify writing projects that students enjoy, especially those that tie the book to their lives. A photographer could bring in photos of real places or staged scenes that reflect the settings or themes. A pair of drama buffs could create and perform a short reading of a key scene using simple props and/or costumes. Include a brief writing or speaking component in which students must refer to passages in the text that influence their decisions as they worked on their project. This should suffice to demonstrate comprehension at a pretty deep level.

Below are some creative projects adaptable to most classes that provide valid measurement information for student records. The caution when assigning differentiated assessments is to monitor how much time each project is taking and to make adjustments so that students can complete your assignments without impinging on the homework time required for other courses. Your colleagues are sure to appreciate your thoughtful consideration of them and the work they are doing with students you share.

Constructing Poems

Invite students to write a found poem. The literary equivalent of a collage, found poetry is often made from newspaper articles, street signs, graffiti, speeches, letters, or even other poems. For an assessment of the novel, students could be required to use specific words and phrases they find in the beginning, middle, and end of the book and arrange these words and phrases into a found but original poem. You could ask them to create three short poems: one each for character, conflict, setting, or for theme.

Students reading *A Day No Pigs Would Die* identify with the boy's physical and emotional growth. They see that he is addressing the same kinds of social fences and facing the same types of adult responsibilities that all adolescents must face. When your students finish reading and begin discussing the entire book, ask them to capture these themes in a poem using exact words and phrases written by the author. Found poems can also be fun to record in audio and video formats and played back to the class, using the principles discussed earlier for digitized presentations.

One poetic variation for this novel is a "Piggy Poem." Students write a fourteen- to sixteen-line poem about *A Day No Pigs Would Die* that portrays incidents, a memorable scene, or a favorite character. They may choose a specific poetic format, one that is structured or unstructured, traditional or new. Your early adolescents may enjoy writing one or more of the following:

- an acrostic
- a lyric poem
- a limerick
- a sonnet
- a free or blank verse poem
- a shape poem
- a rap

For these kinds of poems, evaluate the quality based on linguistic precision—vivid verbs and concrete nouns; fresh figurative language—hyperbole, metaphors, similes, symbols, and so on; and, of course, factual accuracy with the novel. Here is pantoum poem written by a class of seventh-grade students, as summary and reflection of their reading of *Brown Girl Dreaming* by Jacqueline Woodson.

> A girl named Jackie
> In a country divided by race
> Moved from North to south
> Living with the blanket of her grandparent's love
>
> In a country divided by race
> Two siblings and one parent in a long ride "me"
> Living with the blanket of her grandparents' love
> Buried five days a week giving witness to Jehovah
>
> Two siblings and a parent in a long ride "home"
> Anchored in childhood by candy on Friday and ribbons on Sunday
> Buried five days a week giving witness to Jehovah
> Moving gain, New York City, new sibling new life
> A girl named Jackie

CONCLUSION

As you prepare your reading list for the school year, check to make sure you have a variety of topics and genres that provide mirrors, windows, and sliding glass doors. This will ensure that your students are learning more about themselves and about the world while they are meeting the content standards set by your school.

Modern books fit quite well into curriculum designed to be student friendly, culturally relevant to a broad range of students, and also academically vigorous. Adapting ideas from this chapter and using the Internet to locate background information for your chosen book helps to enrich your instruction and capture their own hopes and fears in much the way Robert Peck does in his novel about Rob and his pet, Piggy.

With your careful attention, lessons utilizing and building on students' multimedia skills and their multiple-intelligence learning styles, your student traveling companions soon see that well-told stories can transcend the fences that people put up around themselves and between their communities. Your students discover that fictions, like *A Day No Pigs Would Die*, can help readers erect humane gateways to shared understanding of the diverse experiences that separate and unify us human beings as we seek to live harmoniously in what, at first, was novel territory.

NOTE

1. Robert Newton Peck, *A Day No Pigs Would Die* (New York: Alfred A. Knopf, 1972), 18–19.

Chapter 4

Teaching Classical Fiction: Where the Ghosts of the Past Speak Today

"Are you the spirit, sir, whose coming was foretold to me?"
"I am!"
"Who and what are you?"
"I am the Ghost of Christmas Past."
"Long past?"
"No. Your past. The things that you will see with me are shadows of the things that have been; they will have no consciousness of us."
Scrooge then made bold to inquire what business brought him there.
"Your welfare. Rise and walk with me."[1]

— from *A Christmas Carol*, by Charles Dickens

A ghost. Prophecy. Time travel—long before *The Hunger Games*. Spooky! But also interesting, engaging, and moving. Just the kind of offbeat adventure that most school teens enjoy. Then again, your students are adults in-the-making. They have the capacity to dig deeper than the surface narrative.

Like adults, teens have experienced regret, guilt, and hope. How appropriate that these students should read the works of authors who molded their deepest fears and wonderings into timeless works of fiction. This chapter can help you get started looking back at the classics and helping your learners see what these authors have to say to readers today as they look more closely at the craft and structure of literary writing, thus expanding their travel experience along this journey into more complex literary works.

Unfortunately, your students probably do not immediately see the value in the classics. Young teens sometimes think, "If it's a classic, it must be old!" And, in adolescent logic, if it's old, how can it be good? It is your privilege as their language arts teacher to prepare your students to enjoy what may be the most challenging and rewarding reading experience of their school year.

Charles Dickens's *A Christmas Carol* is the sample story to demonstrate a classroom expedition into the classics. It gives students an opportunity to grapple with a work of exceptional craft and thought whose range helps your students' learning experience extend across genres, cultures, and centuries.

Teaching the classics serves many purposes as you design lessons to help students acquire knowledge and develop skills laid out in the goals of most local, state, and national curricula. The classics that appear on most "must-read" lists teach students about the past, aid in their understanding of the present, and prepare them for the future.

During their excursion back in time and into another place, those you teach will learn that authors of classical fiction use several of the same literary devices you have taught your readers to pay attention to in the short stories and modern novels you already have read together. Of course, no classic is culture-neutral. Consider using *A Christmas Carol* by Charles Dickens because of its universal themes, mindful of the distinctly religious symbols and overtones. Even if you choose other novels that have remained relevant over time, such as those by Alcott, Golding, L'Engle, Lowry, Orwell, Twain, and Lee, the instructional and pacing ideas here will be useful to you.

The different level of attention to content and style of classical writing usually requires that readers slow down and implement comprehension strategies that can be transferred to demanding reading in other content areas. The classics usually provide opportunities to study language and sentence structure in ways that some of the contemporary young adult books do not. Augmenting the study of classical help is the fact that they give students a wealth of knowledge and helps them recognize and understand allusions to these older works that arise in contemporary art, music, and literature. Mainly, many of the classics simply are a joy to teach and read!

In other words, when you have a choice, carefully choose an appropriate balance of classical and contemporary works. These work in tandem to teach the students assigned to you using literary works that give you pleasure to teach.

Even the most challenged readers develop a sense of confidence as learners when they can talk knowledgeably about classical works that their older friends or siblings in honors and advanced placement courses may have read. There is no good reason to deny any the pleasure of the classics.

Carol Jago has written compellingly about keeping the classics in the curriculum in *With Rigor for All: Teaching the Classics to Contemporary Students*. In some situations, just knowing the story will suffice. Depending on the school setting, you may find that some well-written/drawn graphic novels of the classics will be more accessible to your learners. Publishers are

Ebenezer may change your students' minds about reading the classics

providing excellent support materials for classics in graphic novel form like *Great Expectations* by Charles Dickens.

Perhaps the one important reason for studying a classic is to show students that, although times change, people don't. Still, it takes a different kind of preparation to allay apprehension and ease them into understanding and appreciating the classic novel. For one thing, the classic novel is usually set in a time and place completely unfamiliar to contemporary readers. And for another, it likely was written for an audience with entirely different expectations of its writers.

MAKING THE CLASSIC ACCESSIBLE

Right away, make the novel accessible. Timing makes a difference. With *A Christmas Carol*, you could plan to begin the novel in December. Many television, movie, and theatrical performances of this well-known story run during the holiday period, and numerous commercials allude to it. So why not capitalize on the time of year?

The season provides a milieu for reading the text, especially for students whose family may not observe this holiday. Reading this classic may help them understand some of what they see and hear about those who do celebrate Christmas. Another attraction for this book is that teens are surprised that the real story is not "all that long" and that they can comfortably finish it in the three and a half weeks between the traditional Thanksgiving and Christmas vacations.

You may decide on another way to bridge your students to the literature you decide to teach. The classic you choose may work better if you correlate it with the content of course work they are studying in history or science. For example, you may decide to teach the classical thriller *Dr. Jekyll and Mr. Hyde* when they are studying an aspect of genetics in science; *Call of the Wild, The Red Pony, Johnny Tremain,* or *Across Five Aprils* when they study American history.

STUDY PACKETS CAN SUPPORT LEARNING

Another way to ease student concerns about studying a classic novel is to prepare a study packet. When they complete the packet on their own, they experience a sense of accomplishment; the packet also provides a sense of security. This set of prompts and questions need not be collected or graded for anything other than completeness. It simply supplements your teaching and supports student learning.

In addition to, or in lieu of, a journal, the packet becomes a repository for information to study for the quarter or semester exam. Some of the individual class activities that follow are the kinds that readers complete in such a packet—vocabulary work, text-to-world connections, drawings, diagrams, and recording current news that relates to issues raised in the classic novel you choose to teach.

GETTING INTO THE NOVEL: PROVIDING CONTEXT

On the first day of the unit—after the students have made a classics section in their written or digital journals—lay out the context for the novel. In the case of *A Christmas Carol*, it is helpful to explain that in nineteenth-century London, families with leisure time depended on literature for entertainment. They had no radio, television, video, computers, iPads or smartphones, DVD players, or even movie theaters. Readers during this period did not expect the story to end quickly so that they could get on to something else. Reading is how they relaxed after a day of school or work.

Those readers enjoyed imagining what the people and places in the books look and act like; consequently, the authors wrote numerous pages to describe characters' physical appearance and relationships and to establish the setting in terms of time and place. Often these early novels would be read aloud by a family member sitting near a candle, lantern, or oil lamp while the rest of the family sat nearby. The listeners may even have closed their eyes and let the words of the author paint pictures in their minds.

Clearly this was a different time. If you are teaching a fantasy novel, remind them of the different world the author may create. Resist the temptation to show pictures too soon.

Overview before Reading

After distributing the books, give students a few moments to peruse them. Ask them to examine any included graphics. As they begin reading, they may express disagreement with the choices the editors have made to depict characters or places. Their opinions are worth a discussion, so let it happen. It means they are paying attention.

To raise interest in verifying suppositions, ask the students to write down five random page numbers, then turn to those pages and read a few sentences on each. This generates organized randomness. Ask them to predict the significance of these randomly chosen sentences. Teens enjoy guessing and rejoicing when they are right!

As students flip through the pages, invite them to point out what they see that is familiar to them. In *A Christmas Carol*, some recognize the names of Scrooge, Marley, and Tiny Tim. Many have seen television versions of this story with humans, Muppets, or cartoon characters playing the parts. This probably gives students a false sense of security—they know the story. On the other hand, the fact that the story is familiar might entice them to read the "real" one for themselves.

Is there anything unusual about the structure of the novel you have chosen? There is in *A Christmas Carol*; it is not divided into chapters, but into staves.

Staves are similar to the stanzas in traditional hymns or poems. Be sure to clarify formatting differences in the book you are teaching. Some novelists simply use space to show time or scene changes. Point this out to avoid confusion and frustration. Many classic novels have considerably longer descriptive passages than young readers are accustomed to in more modern novels—or there may be no chapter divisions at all!

Creating the Mood to Get Students in the Mood

From the first paragraph, build excitement about the book. Be creative. To help evoke the mood when you begin reading aloud from *A Christmas Carol*, you may dim the classroom lights and ask the students to imagine they are sitting in a room lit by an oil lamp and heated by a fireplace. If your classroom accommodates such an arrangement, pull your chair into a place where they can sit on the floor around you. Read slowly and dramatically. Ask them to visualize the story—to let the author's words "paint a picture" on the canvas of their minds. Yes, they are likely to be wiggly; that's okay. Just pause, give them the "eye," smile and continue reading. For some of them, it may have been years since they last sat and listened to a story.

Sketch to Stretch and Clarify

When you finish a particularly vivid passage, ask the students to draw what they "saw." Some may recognize this as a "Sketch to Stretch" visualization strategy they learned in elementary school. Drawing what they visualize is a way of stretching their imagination. Sharing these quick sketches with partners expands the comprehension of both those drawing and those viewing. It is worth taking the time to get your readers involved on the first day. If you can hook them at this point, they are likely to continue reading with understanding and pleasure.

Of course, to prepare for this dramatic reading, you must practice ahead of time reading the section aloud. Select and read just enough to give them a good sense of the story and yet raise curiosity enough to want to continue reading on their own. While there are professional recordings of many of the classic novels and you may decide to use excerpts from them another time, it is worthwhile for students to hear you read well. It is your voice they hear in their minds when they begin to read on their own, reminding them that you care enough about them to prepare and read so impressively the book the class studies together.

Classical texts like *A Christmas Carol* are generally available in dramatic audio readings. In fact, some classic film clips are accessible free online. During the exposition of the novel, you could select and play them in class just as audio clips without using the video. Check out dramatic readings found on online audio distributors such as iTunes.

Hearing such dramatic readings may intrigue skeptical students to keep reading on their own. Audio clips can also open up initial discussion about the text's setting as reflected in the linguistic codes such as grammar and dialect. Audio versus video requires readers to imagine what the characters and settings look like without preset, pre-conceived visual images.

DECIDING ON VOCABULARY LISTS THAT INCLUDE ACADEMIC WORDS

The vocabulary in classic novels is often difficult and merits direct study. To begin, select eight to ten words from the first section of the novel. Initially, do not get hung up on teaching the words—you are better served by getting into the story right away. For now, quickly give the definitions and move on. The point, of course, is for students to understand enough words to be drawn into the story.

Include a list of suggested vocabulary words in the study packet, along with page references, and encourage students to refer to lists during various lessons. Draw attention to the words during upcoming lessons by posting them on a word wall or having them projected each day as students enter the room. Point out and encourage them to use words they should be adding to their speaking and writing vocabulary.

Reading the words, copying them, seeing them daily, and being encouraged to use them in conversation and writing all are ways to reinforce learning. Some publications of classic novels may have vocabulary already pulled out for you, but you know your learners and may need to tailor this list, personalizing the lessons to fit your school setting.

On subsequent days, as you progress through the novel, you could have pairs of readers look up words in print or digital dictionaries to find the definition that best fits word usage in the novel. Then have students copy appropriate definitions in their notebooks. For this type of vocabulary study there is no need to focus on other meanings of the word.

Have volunteers read the definitions of their assigned words and urge students to make necessary corrections in their own notebooks. Students working on handheld computers may resist this writing assignment thinking they have only to hyperlink the words. Insist that they write because the physical act of writing in and of itself is a heuristic—a way of learning that has long-term retention benefits.

While reading a classic novel you may wish to point out vocabulary words that are important for students to use in their own writing. As a guideline, check the Internet for list of vocabulary that they need to know for academic reading. You can also find graphic organizers showing a variety of ways to have students study new words. Consider asking them to pair words for different reasons: near-synonyms, antonyms, same part of speech, etymology or reminds them of something. What color does this word sound like? Be patient. Be persistent. Learning vocabulary takes time. Make it fun, but not silly. Be imaginative.

Encourage students to keep a list of words that challenge them and then, from these words, assemble a list that the class can work on together. Later in this chapter is a writing assignment requiring readers to incorporate some vocabulary from the novel into a story they write themselves. Consider planning a class meeting during which students use the words as they discuss the story. Yes, there will be giggling; there will also be learning. You may recall the maxim that if you use a new word ten times in a day, it is yours for life. Challenge your teens to test the adage.

WORKING THROUGH THE NOVEL

One way to ensure that your learners are engaged in the novel right from the beginning is to help them grasp firmly the main characters, the setting, and the conflict, or problem to be solved. Then you are ready to dig into serious discussion about character motivation, writing style, use of literary devices, and development of theme. You want to spark thoughtful talking and insightful writing. In this section are examples of ways to increase interest and maintain momentum while studying classic literature, while resisting the temptation to analyze before they complete the first reading.

Accepting Admit Slips

This activity frees students to acknowledge that reading this classic novel is a challenge and that the language and sentence structure are stumbling blocks for them. At the beginning of the next class period, ask each student to write three questions he or she has about section one of the novel you have assigned. They may use their books. While they are writing, you can circulate among them to monitor who is up to date on the reading. Also notice how quickly or slowly they can find passages. This is a hint to whether the passage is familiar or new to them. You may need to adjust your day and give time for students to catch up on the reading.

Once the students write their questions, collect them and assign the next vocabulary exercise. This assignment could be a set of ten words you have

Attentively observe students reading and assist as needed

chosen from the next reading assignment. As they are working in pairs to complete the vocabulary assignment, you can read and organize the admit slips. These questions then form the basis for the discussion of this section and make up the rest of your class time. The point is to help students clarify exposition details so they can continue reading and are less likely to be confused as the story unfolds.

Sampling Study Questions for Classic Novels

You could adapt study questions that fit your novel similar to those that follow for *A Christmas Carol* and can be used as homework or in-class assignment with students working alone or in pairs. For example, you could say: "As you read the story, mark or record answers to the following questions. Then, in your own words, summarize in your reading journal what you've learned from this reading." Then project the following questions or print and distribute them as part of a study packet.

Stave One—"Marley's Ghost"

1. How has Dickens used direct and indirect characterization to reveal the personality of Ebenezer Scrooge? (Indicate page numbers to support answers.)

2. Who is Marley? What part does he play in setting up the conflict of this story?
3. What is the weather like in this stave? How does it affect the setting and mood?
4. List seven to ten verbs to summarize the events of the plot in this stave.
5. What questions do you have about this stave? Ask them at the next class meeting.

Stave Two—"The First of the Three Spirits"

1. At what time does Scrooge awaken?
2. List the places Scrooge is taken by this Ghost. What do we learn about Scrooge?
3. Who uses a candle extinguisher in this stave? What does this character do with it?
4. What does the candle extinguisher symbolize in this stave?
5. What questions do you have about this stave? Ask them at the next class meeting.

Conducting P.I.E. Discussions

Using the questions students write on the admit slips, conduct a discussion of section one of the novel. Read the more frequently asked questions first and direct students to consult their texts to find answers to the questions.

To keep the discussion focused on the author's words, remind students of P.I.E. responses, in which the speaker states the point, illustrates with a reference to a specific incident or sentence from the text, and then explains how that information in the text answers the question. Or you could distribute the admit slips, display a digital timer on your smartboard, or set your timer for five to seven minutes. Assign pairs or triads of readers to search the text and be prepared to share answers with the class when the buzzer rings.

Do not be surprised if discussion on the first section takes two or three full-class periods; the language and style may be more difficult for your students. It is worth a little extra time to clarify the basic elements of character, setting, conflict, and point of view presented in the exposition. However, be alert to the fact that spending too much time dilutes the power of the story. Students lose interest and resist further reading. It is always a balance for teachers. However, the more vigilant you are to what they know and are able to do with this novel, the more likely you are to pace it just right.

For the most part, trust the power of the writing and read quickly, and then go back and discuss. You probably recall times in your education when a teacher or professor spent so much time analyzing the story, chewing it so much that it lost its flavor and you lost interest consuming the tasteless mush on your own. You, of course, want to avoid such blandness in your own teaching.

Assign students to read section two. The number of pages you assign should be based on complexity of the novel you choose and the pace of reading you know they can handle. Be prepared for grumbling, but do not be discouraged if it takes them three or four days to get into the rhythm of classic writing. Instead sustain your enthusiasm; you know the richness of the novel you have chosen to teach them. Need a boost? Now may be a good time to play an audio portion of the novel, or again read another passage aloud yourself. Hearing passages spoken aloud gives students a voice in their minds as they read silently to themselves.

Drawing to Interpret Descriptive Language

Here is an example of how a descriptive writing assignment from *A Christmas Carol* is used; adjust the details based on the book you and your students are reading. You need white paper, colored pencils, pens, or crayons. Encourage each to draw in their packet or journal.

Direct the students' attention to the visual images Dickens creates with his language—vivid verbs, concrete nouns, and humorous details. Ask them to reread the description of the Spirit of Christmas Past, and then as accurately as they can, draw what they visualize.

Circulate among them as they draw, but resist the temptation to comment. Encourage, but do not evaluate. Pay attention to those who go back and reread to find the details and to those who seem to retain the image and quickly begin to draw. Neither is cause for concern. Some may be confident about what they remember; others may not. Some may not have read and are trying to catch up right then and there. Either is fine. More will be ready for the next step.

Once most of the students have completed the drawings, invite two or three of them to draw their pictures on the whiteboard or on large pieces of butcher paper. Because Dickens's descriptions are so detailed, they notice lots of similarities in their drawings.

To focus attention to the language and pattern of the writing, invite volunteers to read aloud passages that appeal to them. This activity stokes their interest, and many become more attentive readers once they see how well they can interpret Dickens's descriptive writing. This version of the "Sketch to Stretch" activity expands and extends comprehension in their reading. Their drawings also help you see what they see when they read.

Enhancing Understanding with Summary Writing

To deepen their understanding and to create a record of key points from the book, teach your learners to write brief reflections similar to those recommended by Tim Shanahan. He suggests:

- summarizing,
- questioning,
- visualizing, and
- monitoring.

You may choose to teach formal summary writing or simply have learners track a sequence of events. Ask them to list the places that the Spirit of Christmas Past takes Scrooge, or in other classic novels where the action moves from place to place.

After students record the locations, they can summarize in a couple of sentences what they infer about the character, what they learn about the character's life—in this case Scrooge's—at each of these places. This unfolding information about character personality and attempts to solve problems naturally leads to conversations about some of the themes in the book.

TEMPTING STUDENTS TO CHEW FOR THEMSELVES

A narrative text is more powerful when it is not dragged out for too long. So when you sense they are relatively comfortable with the structure and style of the text, assign them to continue reading for homework or allot in-class time for reading. Read quickly and then come back and discuss elements of style and the author's use of literary devices. Remember, you are working from a complete reading of the text. You can "see" things they do not notice until they have finished and can reflect on the book as a whole.

Sheridan Blau, in *The Literature Workshop: Teaching Texts and Their Readers*, suggests that teachers enjoy tackling difficult texts for their students. He compares teachers' pre-digesting of literature for students to the mothers chewing food for babies rather than letting children chew for themselves. His point? Don't do that. You may recall your own travels to different areas of the country or to another continent. Though the cuisine usually is different, it often is the fresh meats and vegetables seasoned with exotic spices that make the dining experience both delightful and unforgettable. As you teach your readers to analyze the literature on their own, they begin to experience the flavor of language, joy of reading, and thrill of discovery you may have been hoarding for yourself. Let your students masticate for meaning and savor the flavor of the classical novel.

MODULATING THE PACE FOR READING

As you continue escorting your students along this journey, encourage them to draw an important scene or new character, summarize the events, and discuss the section. Then introduce new vocabulary. Continue assigning reading for homework or for fifteen or twenty minutes during class time. No need to hesitate. You instruct partly by the way you allocate time for classroom activities and skill building. If it is important for them to learn to read independently, you must allot some class time to model and to help them develop that skill.

In addition to modeling silent reading, occasionally, stroll quietly among the readers, carefully observing them as they read. Pay attention to their reading pace. Notice who marks the texts, uses sticky notes, or writes notes in their journal, practicing the skills that you have been teaching. Observe who reads by moving their lips or using their finger to stay focused. Neither is wrong if either helps the student stay focused and read efficiently.

The use of fingers to guide reading is a skill often taught to those who experience dyslexia or who learn speed-reading. It is not necessary to stop any of them from using such reading aids. Just determine who uses them so you can adapt your teaching to accommodate student needs and reading speeds. Not sure what to do? Ask for assistance from a reading specialist. If there is no specialist on staff in your building, ask your department chair, a more experienced colleague, or go online to learn what resources are available in your area, or elsewhere on the Internet.

Posing Intelligent Questions

Continue to ask thought-provoking questions—those that require more than superficial reading to answer. It is at this stage of the story, about half way through the book, you can ask students to predict the outcome. By now the protagonist recognizes that he or she cannot solve the problem alone and may be seeking the assistance of someone or something else. Soon, the protagonist may be challenged to make moral or ethical choices to solve the problem or resolve the conflict. You could ask questions about point of view and how that author's word choices color or flavor the story.

Encouraging students to consider options and to predict ways the characters may address this problem is another way to refocus their attention on characterization and motivation. Do the choices the characters make seem logical to the way the author has developed their personalities? If not, why not? How does this disconnect impact your learners' appreciation of the story? In the same situation, what choices would your students make to solve the problem? Why? Why not? What has happened that is unexpected? Does it make sense?

Using Video Adaptations

Video, picture books, animated cartoons, graphic and comic book adaptations can promote interest, increase comprehension, and lead to worthwhile discussions. Borrow a DVD from the school collection or local library to show portions of the story. You may find appropriate clips online. View the video ahead of time to choose appropriate scenes to show and time their length so you can plan effective use in class.

Look at a variety of adaptations until you find one that you like that serves your purpose for showing it. Characterization? Setting? Pacing? Film making? There is no need to hold off introducing media grammar; just do not spend so much time on the media terms that students are distracted from the novel. This viewing experience can be one to which you refer when you present a more in-depth lesson on media arts.

Before showing the video clip, tell viewers the questions you plan to ask at the end. This helps students focus on some aspects of media grammar—film shots, use of color, timing, screen shots, cuts, and so on. Allow time at the end of the period for them to discuss the director's or artist's choices for depicting character, setting, and action. Ask them how the viewing is different from the reading. Are they surprised, pleased, disappointed? Why? Why not?

Showing visual versions of the novel can help avoid wounding fragile egos. This activity gives students an opportunity to assess and even confirm the assumptions they have been making as they read. And, in a non-embarrassing way, viewing clarifies scenes or passages some may have misunderstood.

You know that classic novels can be challenging reads for today's students, especially those with less experience reading in English or are new to Western culture. So arrange various ways for them to understand the plots and characters. Whether you decide to show video clips, DVD, cartoons, comic book or graphic novel versions, you can be confident that each can supplement and expand their understanding and increase their appreciation for this older, classic work of literature.

If you are teaching a novel that does not have a DVD or other visual format that you can locate, you may use something set in a similar time or place. A careful selection of an alternative resource to view can effectively support your instruction of the classic book you are studying together. Short of time? Post a question in an online teachers' forum. Many participants are eager to share what they know. Another time, you may be the one sharing what you know. The best teaching is shared teaching.

RECOGNIZING STATIC AND DYNAMIC CHARACTERS

About reading two-thirds through the novel is a good time to reflect on and examine the static and dynamic characters in the story. Remember, in fiction, a dynamic character changes as the story unfolds. Usually the static, or unchanging characters serve as foils for the dynamic characters. Ask questions to point out the different types of characters for students for whom this terminology is new or forgotten. Here are a few examples of questions about character development based on *A Christmas Carol*:

1. What specific evidence is there of changes in Scrooge?
2. What is most different about the interaction of this Spirit with Scrooge and that of the other two Spirits?
3. What do you learn about Scrooge based on his interaction with other characters?
4. Through what means do you learn most about Scrooge? Direct or indirect characterization? From what he says or what he does? What others say about him? How others respond to him?
5. Which characters do not change even though they appear in several episodes?

The best literature has clear examples of how and why the characters have changed. Before calling on individuals to verbalize their answers, remind

Writing about reading deepens understanding

them to seek out support for their observations and reference specific passages from the text. Students can write the page numbers in their journals or use sticky notes to mark the sentences they can read aloud and explain why they believe those passages prove the point they wish to make.

Rereading these passages helps to clarify concepts and reinforce vocabulary. Hearing the language reminds readers of ways authors structure sentences to create certain impressions on their readers. No matter what novel you are reading together, there is plenty to talk about on this topic of character motivation and development, use of structure, and choice of vocabulary.

REFLECTING ON THE WHOLE BOOK: SUMMARIZING AND MORE

Dedicate a class period to a summary activity. This may be a time to use the same or a different video version of the book, to show the concluding scenes and ask the students to discuss their responses to the directors' choices. This critical thinking about what they see versus what they read raises their awareness of the power of visual and graphic images to create different responses. You may ask learners to compare what they anticipated in the beginning or predicted in the middle with what they now know at the end of the reading. What caused the change in their understanding? This may also be a good time to consider colors to show characters, setting, and or mood. See Chapter One for ideas regarding colors and arrangements.

MOVING BEYOND THE NOVEL

You are not finished teaching a novel until you have given students opportunities to connect what they have learned with their own life, and with other fiction or nonfiction works. Making connections is not just a higher level of thinking; seeing connections demonstrates why we study rather than merely enjoy literature. One creative way to accomplish this is to have them use their own experience and creativity to write an additional section for the book, an epilogue set sometime in the future. Challenge them to model the style of the author. For *A Christmas Carol*, you could assign the students to write a "Stave Six—Ten Years into the Future."

For whatever novel you decide to teach, the following is a set of guidelines to which you can hold learners accountable when they write epilogues:

- Include at least three characters from the original book.
- Retain their personalities and build on details that have been presented.
- Incorporate seamlessly at least seven words from the vocabulary list.

A great activity to tie up your novel study is a class presentation of these writings of episodes set in the future. Students enjoy hearing what their classmates come up with and talking about what classic novel means to them personally.

Grading Stories the Students Write

You can give a holistic grade for these stories, evaluating them based on their adherence to the prompt. Ask yourself the following questions:

- Have they created a logical epilogue, including three characters that have grown from the descriptions presented in the original work?
- Are the incidents in keeping with the situations introduced by the author?
- Does the vocabulary flow seamlessly (or relatively anyway) into the text of the story? It may or may not, depending on the style and the vocabulary words the students choose to use. If the words are used correctly, go ahead and give full credit. If they all stand out like a palm trees in the desert, lower the grade somewhat.

Connecting Class-Assigned Books with Self-Selected Reading Books

Here is an interesting assignment to encourage additional reading. Have the students read a collection of short stories and write an essay recommending three of the stories to three characters from class readings.

Students can write an epilogue to a classic novel

Reporting on *The New Oxford Book of Ghost Stories* by Dennis Pepper, a seventh grader recommended a story for Scrooge. Here is an excerpt from his essay:

> Another story from *The New Oxford Book of Ghost Stories* is called Snookered. Snookered would be good for Scrooge from a book called *A Christmas Carol* by Charles Dickens. I would recommend that Scrooge read this story because then he would know that it's not just him that are visited by people that they know that have been dead. In Snookered by Catherine Graham, the story is about a man who is playing a game of pool and finds that his friend, that had just died, was helping him win. In *A Christmas Carol,* Scrooge is confronted by his old friend Marley who had died a couple of years ago. In both, they again get to meet their old friends.

This student identified the stories and characters from our class text. He explained why a character from our text might enjoy reading a story about a character from a book that he had read independently. The assignment gave him an opportunity to reflect on our course text and to demonstrate how well he understood the short story he read on his own, both effective and efficient ways to practice and show proficiency in English language arts standards for reading, writing, speaking, listening, and language.

CONCLUSION

You can help your students appreciate classical literature, especially if the related pedagogy and text address the kinds of universal themes that young adults already are pondering. Offer them a variety of options for accessing what may be a more challenging piece of literature. Provide support with vocabulary study, read-alouds—yours or that of professional readers, encourage sketching and drawing, show visual versions, and invite students to connect what they read to their own lives, to what they see around them, and to other literature they have read.

While a book like *A Christmas Carol* can be especially challenging to teach in a multicultural community in which many families are not very familiar with Christmas traditions, it may also prove to be a wonderful window for those who just enjoy the writing of a talented storyteller. As you guide your learners into, through, and beyond classical literature, you also are helping them move closer to reaching the Common Core State Standards for English language arts in reading which says,

> Through wide and deep reading of literature and literary nonfiction of steadily increasing sophistication, learners gain a reservoir of literary and cultural

knowledge, references, and images; the ability to evaluate intricate arguments; and the capacity to surmount the challenges posed by complex texts.[2]

Whatever classic text you select, be sensitive to the cultural nuances as you explore with students the universal themes reflected so well in novels revered so long as the classics.

NOTES

1. Charles Dickens, *A Christmas Carol* (New York: Viking, 2000), 36–37.
2. "English Language Arts Standards » Anchor Standards » College and Career Readiness Anchor Standards for Language." Common Core State Standards Initiative. 2011. http://www.corestandards.org/ (accessed July 4, 2018).

Chapter 5

Opening the Past Imaginatively: Teaching Historical Fiction

> I will always be grateful to her for one thing. She taught me my letters. My mistress, I realize now, like many women of her class, had very little education. She read slowly and laboriously, and it always took her several tearful afternoons to compose a letter to her family in Portugal, or to her nephew in Madrid, a young man who was a painter. Yet Mistress had a great deal of practical wisdom, and she knew many things because she trusted her judgment and cultivated her memory.[1]
>
> —from *I, Juan de Pareja*, by Elizabeth Borton de Treviño

Three sentences. A mistress, a slave, a painter. Tearful afternoons, practical wisdom, and judgment. From Spain to Italy—and beyond. All brought alive through the magic of one work of historical fiction transports twenty-first-century teens to Renaissance Europe. Three sentences and thousands of miles spanning hundreds of years. Here is an entirely engaging education in one novel of historical fiction thanks to a splendid writer like Borton de Treviño.

Several authors write historical fiction, and there may be a title on your list to teach. With the ideas here and this accessible novel you can have a great time exploring the past. You will also meet the academic needs of your students and the curriculum and standards for English language arts that may be goals at your school for reading, writing, speaking, listening, viewing, and using technology.

Not only is teaching historical fiction fun, but it also is an excellent way to integrate the English language arts with other subjects like social studies, science, and the arts. Like tour companies that include visits to museums or ancient towns as part of their travel packages, you can do the same with your curriculum.

Interdisciplinary planning can divide the work and multiple benefits

Consider collaborating with colleagues in another department. In this case, choose a literary work that introduces or reinforces an historical period or explores some scientific concept your common students are learning in one of those content areas. You can create together a course of study that meets the requirements of your content area and in state and national standards, and presents the kinds of integrated lessons so critical to a successful program for adolescents. Such cross-curricular study helps students see and make connections across the disciplines. It also makes for an enriching experience for you.

WONDERING WHY THIS HISTORICAL NOVEL?

I, Juan de Pareja, by Elizabeth Borton de Treviño, is written as an autobiography from the point of view of Juan, a real African slave inherited by Diego de Velázquez, the court painter for King Philip IV of Spain who reigned in the seventeenth century. Juan became the assistant and a friend to Velázquez and later an accomplished painter in his own right. One of Juan de Pareja's paintings hangs in the Prado Museum in Madrid, Spain, and Velázquez' painting of Juan is in the New York Metropolitan Museum of Art. See images of both paintings at art sites on the Internet.

If you are looking for an engaging book that expands your reading list to include works from, and about, other cultures, this one works. It may become an immediate favorite to teach if you are inspired by a colleague like Suzanne who had been "a closet art historian."

Suzanne pointed out that Velázquez' work reflects four schools of European art. Descriptions in the book introduce readers to specific fifteenth- and sixteenth-century painters' artwork and the distinctive characteristics of chiaroscuro, baroque, realism, and idealism. Borton de Treviño writes so clearly students hardly realize how much they are learning. But you can assure that they do so from the very beginning by letting them help build the foundation as they conduct simple research on the historical period.

Student Research of Historical Settings

The novel, *I, Juan de Pareja*, is set during the Renaissance. In the novel, Rubens (1577–1640), the famous Flemish painter, visits the Spanish Court, and Velázquez travels to Italy to purchase art for King Philip. Imagine the budget!

This novel also talks about friendships—a topic students also love to talk about. The characters are faced with ethical dilemmas that can elicit lively student conversations about issues of right and wrong. Studying historical fiction gives students an opportunity to meet such English language arts standards for reading works that offer profound insights into the human condition and serve as models for students' own thinking and writing.[2]

Have students research historical settings

The premise of this novel is the fact that the painting *Las Meniñas*, in which Velázquez includes a portrait of himself, has the Cross of Santiago painted onto his garment in a style quite different from his own. Borton de Treviño's tale attempts to explain who painted this cross and why anyone would do so. That is a good reason to display a copy of *Las Meniñas* in your classroom while you and your students study this particular historical novel. Images of famous artwork like this are readily available on a range of websites and in books with Renaissance art found in most libraries. If you choose a different novel, consider assembling and having on hand photos and images of the historical setting of that literary work.

IMMERSING STUDENTS INTO THE NOVEL

Begin explaining to students the features of historical fiction and the fact that they are going to be reading one. Share with them that historical fiction may include real people, places, and events. Following Louise Rosenblatt's reader-response approach, encourage students to look for the familiar, even in a piece of historical fiction. Susan Zimmerman and Chryse Hutchins, in *Seven Keys to Comprehension: How to Help Your Kids Read It and Get It*, use different terminology but also urge teachers to have students make connections when reading literature. These educators advocate such relationships as

- text to self (between the novel and their own lives);
- text to text (among the people, places, and incidents in the novel);
- text to text (between this and other literature students have read); and
- text to world (between this book and historical or current events).

If you choose a novel in collaboration with a colleague from another content area, add text to study in history or text to study in science, or whatever the other content area is.

When you teach a work of historical fiction, it is important to set the scene. For *I, Juan de Pareja*, give a brief overview of the Renaissance period, an era whose style in art history began in Rome, Italy, and spread through Europe from 1450 to 1600. Following the dark ages, this was a period of intense revival in all areas of math, science, arts, and humanities.

Presenting Oral Reports
Gives Overview of People and Events

To help set the stage for students to acquire a richer sense of the historical period and to practice their research skills, you can let them look for information about the real people, places, and events of the period in which the novel is set and report to the class what they learn.

Consider assigning them to use the Internet or an ordinary general encyclopedia to learn about the people of the golden age that Borton de Treviño mentions in her "Foreword," such as Galileo, Rembrandt, and Sir Walter Raleigh. Most of the names on this list are so well known that students have little difficulty locating facts for a brief two- to three-minute informative speech. The same is likely to be true for the novel you choose since historical novels tend to be written about famous events, well-known places, or legendary people.

Depending on your students' access to resources, you may decide to spend a week on this assignment, allowing in-class time for research, writing, and practice. To reduce innocent plagiarism, you may wish to include mini-lessons on note-taking, summarizing and documentation, and making citations. And it is a good idea to assign students to use time at home to practice their delivery, perhaps in front of two adults who sign a form confirming that they have heard the speech. This also is a way to let families and friends know what their child or friend is learning.

Research for Real Purposes

This mini-assignment has a real purpose for conducting simple research, collaborating with a peer, practicing speech writing, and giving oral reports. If it is not realistic to expect your students to complete this assignment at home, allot in-class time for pairs of students to give their speeches to each other or recruit faculty and staff at your school to be listeners. You may be surprised how many school support staff members are delighted to play a part in the academic education of students they serve as secretaries, janitors, bus drivers, and cafeteria workers.

Check for Gender Representation and Cultural Relevance

As you prepare for teaching *I, Juan de Pareja*, notice many of the names in the "Foreword," such as Galileo, Rubens, and Shakespeare are familiar, but none are women. But as you conduct background research on artists of this period, you do learn that two female artists should be included: Artemisia Gentileschi and Elisabetta Sirani.

Both Gentileschi and Sirani were talented artists whose work is equal to that of their male contemporaries. Add their names to your list along with other noteworthy names of women of the Renaissance. If you choose another book and decide to do this assignment, carefully check for and include women of renown from that historical period and other cultures whose contributions are key to events in that time period.

It may be a little more difficult for your students to locate information about women of the Renaissance, other than Joan of Arc. Nevertheless, students should be able to locate online information about (1) Elisabetta Sirani, (2) Artemisia Gentileschi, (3) Grace O'Malley, (4) Christina of Sweden, and (5) Gracia Mendes Nasi, all of whom were active in arts and government during that period.

For ease in assigning topics, simply have students pull for numbers 1–18 or more (based on the number of names on the list). Those who have the same number can research the same person, and then work together to decide how to best make their presentation. Each presentation should include the following information based on the five Ws and an H: who, what, when, where, why, and how. Whatever list of people you offer your students should reflect both genders and cultural, social, economic, and political incidents representative of the historical setting of your book.

SAMPLE ASSIGNMENT SHEET
FOR AN ORAL PRESENTATION
BASED ON RENAISSANCE PERSONAGES

1. Use a print or online encyclopedia to find the answers to the following questions about the person about whom you are assigned to give an oral report:

   - Who is the person?
   - What is he or she famous for doing?
   - When was he or she born?
   - Where was he or she born? Locate the country on a world map.
   - Why is his or her work, invention, discovery, and so on important in contemporary society?
   - How was his or her work, invention, discovery, and so on viewed during his or her lifetime?

2. Record the information that tells where you get your facts. Include:

   - author (if one is listed)
   - title of article or encyclopedia entry
   - title of encyclopedia or website and its URL
   - number of volumes (if applicable)
   - city where published
   - publisher
   - year the book was published, article posted, or website updated
   - date you accessed the website with information you are using

3. Write a one-page summary that highlights what you learned to make an engaging informative speech. Include a picture, if one is available. (A written summary of 250 words takes about two minutes to speak.)

If your students are tech savvy and have access to resources, consider challenging them to prepare slides for *pecha kucha* presentations. These are based on a Japanese concept of twenty slides paced to advance every twenty seconds during which someone narrates, making a six-minute, forty-second presentation.

For example, you might subdivide the task among four or five groups. Each would be responsible for four or five slides each. Depending on the book you choose, this subdividing could be into categories. For example, for the *Juan* book, the subdivisions could be art, science, math, and religion. Let students decide. Save the slides and show them again before the test or exam.

Validating Student Research

To expand their knowledge, extend their recall, and validate the significance of their classmates' research, assign students to keep notes as their peers speak. At the end of the unit or semester, include questions based on these reports. This provides an opportunity to demonstrate on an exam what they have learned during their study of the historical novel.

While they are researching and once they have presented their oral reports, keep the list of names visible, either written on the board, on a poster, or projected on a screen when students enter the classroom. Because they are likely to encounter these names as they study history, science, and art, the assignments in this unit support many interdisciplinary curricula. Keeping such a word wall with these names is another effective way to reinforce valuable new information students learn from reading for this mini-research presentation.

Symbols Extend Fact Retention

Symbols and images help students remember details. In their journal section set aside for notes about this historical novel, ask them to create a chart on which they list the names of the historical personages with space to include five W and H facts as well as a column in which to draw in symbols or images. During the presentation by classmates, have students write facts they hear. At the end of the presentations, as you review this information, invite them to recommend appropriate symbols or images to serve as memory aids.

For example, for Galileo, someone may suggest a telescope; for Moliere, the happy and sad face drama masks; for Isaac Newton, a stick figure sitting under an apple tree; for Joan of Arc, a woman with a sword. Deciding appropriate symbols is another way to teach to the multiple intelligences your students have, those who learn best by drawing and those who learn best by viewing. Consider asking one of the more artistic youngsters to draw the symbols for the class to copy. This can be a fine time for you to stand aside and let them shine.

VARIATION REINFORCES LEARNING

During the first couple of weeks the class reads and discusses the novel, schedule a four- or five-minute review of the historical personages at the beginning of each period. One day you could project or show the symbol(s) for ten or more of the historical figures and have students name the person(s) and something for which each is famous. Another day read the names and ask them to draw the symbol or write a fact about the person.

To avoid having to collect and grade these quickie quizzes, just conduct "honor" checks. While students are writing their responses, pick up your grade book and have it ready to record how they did, immediately following the quiz.

Since the purpose of this activity is to give students a daily opportunity to show they are learning about these famous Renaissance personages, you want to make the activity low-key. Therefore, immediately following the quiz, go over the answers and ask students to indicate how many they missed, using their fingers held close to their chests so that only you can see them. Then just record a check-plus, check, or check-minus instead of a letter grade. If someone misses more than five, enter a minus sign.

Commend them all for their work and move to the next activity for the day. Your daily checks encourage them to study their notes, and by the second week most students are able to identify these famous figures and recall a pertinent fact about each one.

Occasionally some of your students extend the assignment on their own and bring in articles or ads from the newspapers or magazines that allude to or mention the people on your list or show some symbol of the times. Depending on where you are teaching, you may ask them to search through the telephone book, the local newspaper, or online websites to see how many products and companies carry these Renaissance names, or names of people or places in the book you are studying.

Quickly record quiz grades and move on with lesson

INVITING STUDENTS TO SUPPLEMENT WITH VISUAL DISPLAYS

Set aside a space in the classroom, hang up a blank poster board, and encourage students to bring in examples. They can add these examples to a poster that all can view during your study of the historical fiction novel. For, *I, Juan de Pareja*, you could label the poster "Renaissance Today" and watch as a collage of student contributions emerge. You could have students add their findings to a gallery you set up in an online class folder just for this purpose, or, in the image of a school year being an extended tour, keeping a travel album on people you meet and places you visit.

These are just ways to have students pay attention to the world around them, think about what they are reading, and contribute to the learning environment they share with you.

OFFERING EXTRA CREDIT—YES AND NO

Yes, it is fine to offer extra credit when students find the names of the people mentioned in your text in their history or science texts or in the newspaper.

You want to ensure that students are making connections but not simply finding the names and earning unwarranted extra credit.

To help control dependence on the extra-credit option, limit the percentage of extra points students may earn each marking period to about 5 percent. These extra points can help a student who has had a slow start to make up for homework points missed earlier in the marking period, or to make up for a test or quiz taken when the student had been tired, ill, or distracted by some personal issue. With most students, it doesn't take much for them to have an off day!

Extra points, however, should neither be so weighty that they make it unnecessary for students to earn passing grades on required curriculum content nor should such work take up time they should be giving to learning basic course content materials or skills. Most important, extra-credit points should not require extra work for you, the teacher.

All extra-credit work should be submitted and recorded at least a week before the marking period ends. This early cutoff date reduces the temptation for students to misdirect their attention from learning and showing knowledge of required course content and skill acquisition just to raise their quarter grade. Enforcing this early cutoff date also preserves time for you to grade those assignments needed to determine grades for that marking period.

WORKING THROUGH THE NOVEL

If possible, teach the historical novel in the spring. By this time, your students already have studied the structure of fiction and several short stories that illustrate the elements of fiction and they know the literary devices authors use to enhance the storytelling. Your maturing teens know to set up a section in their journals for this new kind of novel, and to write notes as you present facts about the period in which this particular historical novel is set. When you begin your unit, just remind them that historical novels are fiction, with plotlines followed in much the same way as short stories.

By spring, your students know to pay attention to facts revealed in the exposition, but you may need to review ways to mark their texts or to take notes in their journals. For example, you could have them use a pencil to circle the name of each character when first introduced in the reading. Then underline words or phrases that identify that character. If they are using an electronic version, they can highlight and annotate as you have taught for this environment.

Offering Options for Marking Texts

If students are not allowed to write in their texts, they can list names of new characters in their reading journals and include page numbers and a few words or phrases the author uses to identify those characters. Then ask them to remain alert as they continue reading to see if or how the author rounds out the characters through direct and indirect characterization. By this time in the school year, your students know that the protagonist is a dynamic character, so they are watching to see what encounters bring about the change in this character, from the beginning through the challenge of the conflict and on to the falling action and resolution.

Students can identify the setting by putting a rectangle around words and/or phrases that indicate time(s) and place(s), or students can record this information in their journals. This kind of marking or writing forces students to slow down a bit. It also helps them get to know people and places in the book, and these readers are less likely to become confused as the action intensifies and conflict complicates. Because *Juan* is written as an autobiography, students quickly notice that the point of view is first person and can predict that the major problem to be solved is that of growing up and surviving the challenges Juan encounters during his lifetime.

As with all direct instruction of reading, my friend, Carol Jago reminds teachers to help students refine how they examine literature without destroying their confidence as readers. Teaching students to be active readers increases reliance in their own ability to understand whatever they read, whenever they read, and for whatever purpose they read. Paying attention to the craft and structure of the genre leads students toward the curriculum standard goals you are charged to help them reach.

Stimulating Interest in Styles of Painting

After reading chapter 5, "In Which Rubens Visits Our Court," you can introduce students to four styles of art reflected in the book and prominent in the Renaissance: chiaroscuro, baroque, realism, and idealism. This prepares them to understand later book-related discussions about art. Keep in mind that art often reflects the social, economic, and political milieu of the times in which the artists live. So even if you are teaching a different novel, it still is worthwhile to bring in photos, art work, artifacts, or articles. They all can give a richer sense of the historical period in which your novel is set.

The school media center likely has many resources you can borrow for use in your classroom. The Library of Congress maintains an extensive collection of photographs readily accessible on the Internet to you and your students. Encourage them to explore and bring in artwork and photos relating to the content of your work of historical fiction.

You could adapt your presentation of art terms like this. Prepare a handout with the information you want them to reference. Use a computer slide program to present visual examples of each style. During the slide presentation, read some of the narration that defines and illustrates key terms: chiaroscuro, baroque, realism, and idealism. In the section of the companion website for this book is the *I, Juan de Pareja* PowerPoint presentation prepared to supplement this unit. (See http://teachingenglishlanguagearts.com.)

If you and your students are enjoying this adventure with art, consider letting them demonstrate their new knowledge of art. Create a scavenger hunt during which they find examples of various paintings and styles in library books with collections of Renaissance art. You can do the same with historical novels set in other times and places. The National Archives has valuable resources on American artists. Artcylopedia.com has searchable pages that make the hunt less daunting for you. Let students post what they find in the class online folder or create an electronic slide presentation that they show one day in class.

If you are teaching a different historical novel and would like to incorporate a visual arts component, do so. Many art terms apply to painting styles of other historical periods. Among the historical novels that work well for this kind of study are

- *Across Five Aprils* by Irene Hunt
- *Bud, Not Buddy* by Christopher Paul Curtis
- *Echo* by Pam Muñoz Ryan
- *Esperanza Rising* by Pam Muñoz Ryan
- *Code Talker: A Novel about the Navajo Marines of World War Two* by Joseph Bruchac
- *Girl with the Pearl Earring* by Susan Vreeland

The Library of Congress website (loc.gov) and numerous open access websites provide historical photographs to enhance the study of each of these titles. The loc.gov site also has sound recordings of real people from American history. Include auditory resources to support students who learn best by listening to real people talk about their lives and times. Hearing these recordings can make these historical personages come alive and more culturally relevant for all your students.

Connecting Geography and Map Study

Velázquez and Juan make two trips from Spain to Italy; the story gives their itinerary. Ask students to locate the places on a map and follow the journey by marking the places they visit. You could print out copies of a blank map that includes outlines of Europe with France, Spain, and Italy, or of the places mentioned in your book. Consider those interactive GPS maps available online. *The Watsons Go to Birmingham* by Christopher Paul Curtis is another fine travel novel written as historical fiction.

Using Google Maps for Historical Literature

If you have access in the classroom or a media center to the Google Maps website you can view the following with students:

- current street-view images of historical sites;
- traditional, satellite-image, and topographical maps of locales; and
- website previews of sites about historical buildings, events, and people.

For those reading *Juan*, this map work gives students a sense of the distance between towns and the kind of topography the two characters had to cross to get to the Mediterranean Sea and then on to their destinations in Italy. Since map reading is a skill most students are expected to acquire, asking them to refer to and use maps while studying in your class provides opportunities to practice that skill as they expand their understanding on what is going on in the novel they are reading with you.

EXPLORING FRIENDSHIP: A MULTILAYERED THEME

Elizabeth Borton de Treviño artfully describes friendships between (1) King Phillip and his court painter, (2) the court painter and his slave, (3) the apprentices and a slave, (4) a dwarf and a slave, and (5) a male and a female slave. These relationships are ready-made springboards for discussions about the nature of friendship.

You could get the discussion off the ground by writing the word *friend* in the center of the whiteboard, on a poster, or on something you can project for all to see as you write. Then ask students to brainstorm for words to describe a friend. Without commenting, list their answers around the word *friend* forming a web-like cluster.

Next, ask them to open their journals to the section on this novel, and do a quick-write on friends or friendship. Set your timer and write along with them. Having them write nonstop for three or four minutes describing their concept or experience with friends usually elicits a level of honesty that may be missing in more prepared writing. They may write about a friendship that went well, one that dissolved, or one they wish existed.

Then invite a few students to read aloud what they have written, respecting their privacy if they decline. Unedited writing sometimes reveals emotions too raw to share in public. So, again, honor the choice to pass. While they are writing, you could create a word cloud of the terms they used and project it to sum up your discussion. See Wordle.com.

Round out the lesson by asking students to write about the friendships they notice are developing in your novel. (1) Which surprised them? (2) Which do they think will develop, continue, or end? Why? Why not? To help students go beyond a simple listing of facts in their speaking and writing, encourage them to continue using P.I.E. paragraph format—where they answer the questions by stating their point, using specific incidents from the text to illustrate that point, then explaining the reasons they believe the incidents show that the friendship identified begins, continues, or ends.

Because P.I.E. writings are more objective than quick-writes, students often are more willing to share them. In fact, some might disagree and even debate their differences about friendship. To keep them focused on the text and to practice considering perspectives of others, challenge them to take an opposing stance they can support with evidence from the book. Doing so, they experience what it is like to give serious consideration to an alternative point of view—good practice for developing open minds about others.

WRITING ABOUT AND DISCUSSING ETHICAL ISSUES

The Association for Middle Level Education (AMLE) recommends that teachers address ethical issues while developing curricula. One of its publications even argues that any "curriculum design that does not provide opportunities and support for students to do 'right things' along with the significant adults in their lives is sadly incomplete."[3] A unit of study based on novels like *I, Juan de Pareja* provides such opportunities. Juan and the other characters in the book are faced with a number of ethical choices related to slavery, honesty, and loyalty. Consider the presence of ethical issues in the readings you choose to round out your curriculum.

The word *ethics* normally refers to defining and using standards of right and wrong, moral and immoral conduct. Ethics also involves analyzing situations in which people have to address moral conduct, duty, and judgment—making right but often tough decisions. Several of the characters in this autobiographical novel are faced with just such choices. As your students read about them, they may identify with these situations even if they disagree with the characters' choices having to do with selling humans as slaves or using mentally and physically challenged persons to entertain the royal children.

Very likely equally evocative topics arise in the book you choose to teach. Some raging debates may arise among students when you challenge them to consider the actions and attitudes expressed in the stories they read. Do what you can to monitor but not squelch heated but respectful exchanges of ideas, and let them know that it is perfectly all right to agree to disagree.

RESPONDING HOLISTICALLY TO LITERATURE

Fran Claggett, in *Drawing Your Own Conclusions: Graphic Strategies for Reading, Writing, and Thinking*, wrote that teachers often dissect literature so minutely that students lose sight of the work as a whole. She recommends using art and graphics to give readers an opportunity to "make it whole" again. Here is another opening to assign art, music, or poetry writing for that purpose: to help students reassemble the parts of the story and to see the novel as a whole work of literature. One assignment asks students to compose a narrative poem, similar to a ballad, in which they tell the whole story in quatrains. In this case, have them include at least five four-line stanzas to account for the exposition, rising action, climax, falling action, and resolution of the story.

You may find your students enjoy writing a pantoum poem as a way to summarize the historical novel they study. You saw an example in Chapter Three that Anne Brown's seventh graders drafted after reading *Brown Girl Dreaming* by Jacqueline Woodson. Here is a poem written by another class of seventh-grade students. They had finished reading *A Farewell to Manzanar*, by John Houston and Jeanne Watasuki Houston, an autobiographical novel about Japanese internment during World War II. Note the instructions are in Italics.

Choose a Character, Situation, or Theme and Write a Pantoum Poem

Write your title at the top of your final draft and at the bottom the title and author of the book you read. Punctuate that book title correctly and edit for grammar, spelling, and usage.

Begin by writing four original lines:

(1) When I was seven.
(2) My family was evacuated.
(3) We rode a bus.
(4) To Manzanar.

Repeat lines two and four, and add lines five and six to expand ideas introduced in lines two and four, like this:

(2) My family was evacuated.
(5) Only forty-eight hours to prepare, then...

(4) To Manzanar.
(6) We rode in shock, but together.

Repeat lines five and six, and add lines seven and eight to expand ideas mentioned in lines five and six, like this:

(5) Only forty-eight hours to prepare.
(7) Mama, stressed and frustrated, broke all the dishes.
(6) We rode in shock, but together.
(8) Together, except for Papa.

Finally, repeat lines one, three, seven, and eight in this order:

(7) Mama, stressed and frustrated, broke all the dishes.
(3) We rode a bus.
(8) Together, except for Papa.
(1) When I was seven.

The class's final poem, then, read

> *When I was seven*
> *My family was evacuated.*
> *We rode a bus*
> *To Manzanar.*
>
> *My family was evacuated.*
> *Only forty-eight hours to prepare, then*
> *To Manzanar.*
> *We rode in shock, but together.*
>
> *Only forty-eight hours to prepare, then*
> *Mama, stressed and frustrated, broke all the dishes.*
> *We rode in shock, but together.*
> *Together, except for Papa.*
>
> *Mama, stressed and frustrated, broke all the dishes.*
> *We rode a bus*
> *Together, except for Papa.*
> *When I was seven.*

If you choose to teach historical fiction at the end of the school year, your students already will have had an in-depth poetry unit during which they learned that writing can be a poem—even if it does not have a set rhyme or rhythm pattern—as long as the writing "convey[s] a vivid and imaginative sense of experience, especially by the use of condensed language."[4]

ASSIGNING ALTERNATIVE END-OF-NOVEL ASSIGNMENTS

The following are particularly useful kinds of creative, open assignments to offer at the end of a unit. They allow you to see what your students have learned in ways that may not have been revealed in response to earlier assignments. Students are free to choose their idea and structure to demonstrate what they know. Possibilities include:

- create a melody for each of three or four of the main characters (à la Darth Vader theme from *Star Wars*);
- bring in samples of music that reflect key scenes (like mood music);
- bring in three or four different published songs that have lyrics that could have been sung by three or four different characters; or
- create original music for any of the three previously mentioned situations.

Ask students to write a page or two in which they explain the reasons for their choices and to indicate the page(s) of the text that support their choices for music.

One parent complained that I was "dumbing down" the curriculum when I allowed students to use artistic projects to show their understanding about the characters and their relationships and roles in the literature. However, after visiting my classroom to see the students' artwork, he noticed and acknowledged the sophisticated levels of comprehension they reflected. He was so impressed with the depth, breadth, and creativity of the work that he asked if he could sit in the class for the remainder of that unit!

You can be sure your alternative assignments are well designed and serve as successful alternative assessments if you

- determine in advance what you want to learn about your students,
- tell students the knowledge on which they are being evaluated, and
- give them options to show that knowledge in their dominant intelligence.

CONCLUSION

Art illuminates
lessons we teach our students
and they understand.

—Anna J. Small Roseboro

Elizabeth Borton de Treviño's *I, Juan de Pareja* is a rich source of multidisciplinary material for teaching. It provides a luxury side trip on this school year journey, the kind one would experience visiting a historical dig while on a trip to the modern high-rise city of Kuala Lumpur. Like other works of historical fiction, you could teach it simply as fiction, or you can look at it as a way to have students look at the past to see the present and perhaps at ways to change the future.

Assignments accompanying this particular novel give your students opportunities to refine their research skills; hone their speaking abilities; discover Renaissance people, places, and events; view art by renowned painters; and write about and discuss issues of friendship and ethics. They also meet the majority of the English language arts standards set by your course curriculum.

Like the mistress described in *I, Juan de Pareja*, your students may at first find that they read slowly and laboriously and have to spend tearful afternoons writing. But once they have the pleasure of getting to know about people and places, delving into another time period through reading, writing, viewing, and discussing ideas to which they can relate today, they feel more confident and competent in demonstrating their refined Common Core skills and the personal challenges they face in the century in which they live.

NOTES

1. Elizabeth Borton de Treviño, *I, Juan de Pareja* (New York: HarperCollins, 1993), 6.
2. *Core Standards*. 2011. http://www.corestandards.org/ (accessed July 4, 2018).
3. Chris Stevenson, "Curriculum That Is Challenging, Integrative, and Exploratory." In *This We Believe . . . and Now We Must Act*, ed. Thomas Owen. Erb (Westerville, OH: National Middle School Association, 2001), 63.
4. *Houghton-Mifflin College Dictionary*, 1986.

Chapter 6

Taking T.I.M.E. to Teach Poetry

>Words stir me
>When I hear them,
>When I read them,
>When I write them,
>When I speak them.
>
>Words urge me
>To keep listening
>To keep reading
>To keep writing
>To keep speaking.
>
>Let me hear you,
>so I can know you.
>Let me speak,
>so you can know me.
>
>Prodigiously stirring words
>help me know you.
>And viscerally urging words
>help me know me.
>
>—"Words, Words, Words," by Anna J. Small Roseboro.

For some reason, teens are apprehensive about studying poetry. They believe there is a key or secret code to understanding poetry and only teachers have the key to decipher that code. Experienced readers know that is not the case; it is a matter of understanding the genre and approaching poetry in a different

Planning a poetry unit need not overwhelm you

way—paying special attention to poets' careful selection and arrangement of words.

The lessons in this chapter are designed to provide you and your students with a set of strategies that can help them approach, read, understand, analyze, and write about classical, contemporary, structured, and free-verse poetry. They will be reading closely and developing English language arts anchor skills related to reading, writing, speaking, listening, and viewing while using technology for learning, publishing, and showing what they know.

PREPARING TO TEACH POETRY

Scrounge as many books of poetry as you can. Look for them at the school or neighborhood library, your department library, and borrow from your colleagues. If several of you are teaching poetry at the same time, you may wish to borrow a library cart so you can merge your poetry collections and move the cart easily among your rooms. To make this a really rich experience for your students, have a ready trove of poems for them to mine during their study of poetry.

If your students have access to technology at home or at school, assemble a list of age-appropriate websites to post as a hyperlinked list on your webpage so they can access them quickly. See the companion website at www.

teachingenglishlanguagearts.com for a list of collections and links to inspect and select as resources you can make available for students to peruse and use. Even if you are in a high-tech setting, lots of print books should still be on hand.

USING A POEM TO INTRODUCE POETRY ANALYSIS

Begin with a short poem explaining the process. Consider "Unfolding Bud" by Naoshi Koriyama. Post or project it where students can see it on the first day of direct poetry reading instruction. This poem provides a useful metaphor for students' experience when reading and seems to allay some anxiety about understanding poetry. You may also hand out copies, but at first do not read the poem aloud. Instead, without saying anything, let them consider it for a couple of minutes. Sometimes silence gives space for student learning.

Now use a multiple readings format; it works like this. Ask students to read the poem silently, paying attention to the punctuation, and marking words or phrases that catch their attention. Next, read the poem aloud yourself. Then do one or both versions of "jump in" oral reading. In version one, invite students to read a line at a time. Let them volunteer and begin reading on their own. At the end of the line, stop, and without raising their hands, different students read, stopping at the end of each succeeding line until the end of the poem.

Students are likely to giggle when more than one of them begins reading aloud at the same time. Just have them start over and encourage those who jump in at the same time to listen to each other and read together as one voice. It usually takes three or four false starts before they get the idea and are comfortable reading aloud this way. Others will continue jumping in to read in this way until the end of the poem.

In version two of jump-in reading, the first student reads and stops at the first mark of punctuation (comma, semicolon, period, question mark, etc.). Another student, without raising his or her hand, continues reading until the next punctuation mark. Again, if more than one student begins reading at the same time, have them begin again, listening to one another and read as one voice.

Relax and allow the pauses between readers to be moments of resonation and reflection. False starts encourage students to pay attention to the words, lines, and punctuation, and thus expand their understanding of the poem. The different single and blend of multiple voices resonate meaning and message.

This first day is a good time to talk about the value of multiple readings and why they often are necessary for understanding this condensed form of literature. The "Unfolding Bud" poem is a great conversation starter for this topic because Koriyama compares reading a poem to watching a water lily bud unfold. It takes time, but is worth the wait.

MESSAGE, RATHER THAN MEANING

When teaching poetry, resist the temptation to ask students what the poem "means." This phrase incorrectly suggests there is only one meaning for a poem. The phrase "what it says" encourages them to look at the individual words and respond with a literal meaning, which can be the first step to analyzing poetry. The subsequent steps include determining whether the poem is saying something about a bigger issue or idea and whether the poem is speaking metaphorically.

Some poets may not have begun writing their poem about big universal issues; they may have written simply to re-create a very personal incident, observation, or experience. Yet, when read by others, their poem speaks to readers about issues quite different from literal ideas originally intended. Often these bigger ideas do not emerge or manifest themselves on first or second readings. "Unfolding Bud" closes with the lines "over and over again," which suggests that poetry is somewhat different from other genres and, more often than not, requires multiple readings to understand.

Some poets, like Quincy Troupe, are aware that poems can mean more than the words on the page. Share with your students these excerpted stanzas from his poem, "My Poems Have Holes Sewn into Them." Have fun with the unusual way the words are organized. Note particularly the last words in each line, the punning, and the use of the ampersand sign instead of the word "and." How do these impact the reading? (Won't "ampersand" be fun to teach middle school students?)

> my poems have holes sewn into them
> & they run, searching for light
> at the end of tunnels, they become trains
> or at the bottom of pits, they become blackness
> or in the broad, winging daylight
> they are words that fly
> . . . .
>
> my poems have holes sewn into them
> & their voices are like different keyholes
> through which dumb men search for speech, blind
> men search for sight
> words, like drills, penetrating sleep

> keys unlocking keyholes of language
> words giving sight to blind peoples eyes
> . . .
>
> my poems have holes sewn into them
> & they are spaces between worlds
> are worlds themselves
> words falling off into one another
> colliding, like people gone mad, they space out
> fall, into bottomless pits, which are black
> holes of letters that become words
> & worlds, like silent space
> between chords of a piano
>
> — Quincy Troupe[1]

Reading Poems in Alternative Ways

If you would rather not use "jump-in" reading to introduce the unit, slowly read the poem aloud yourself, allowing time for the words to make their impact. Then ask a student to read the poem according to the punctuation, rather than just stopping at the end of each line. This second reading helps them focus on the fact that poems sometimes include punctuation and that the punctuation serves the same functions as that used in prose.

Punctuation clarifies the meaning of words organized in a particular order. It still is beneficial to have a third student read the poem, who by this time may have an idea of what the poet may be trying to express. This third reader may choose to emphasize different words or read at a different pace and thus offer a third level of understanding. Either approach—jump-in reading or multiple readings—demonstrates the value of repetition to allow a poem time to reveal itself to readers and listeners.

DEFINING POETRY: A FOUNDATION FOR DISCUSSION

Now, on the first day of the unit, is a prime time to explore a definition of poetry, this distinctive genre of literature that sometimes baffles new readers and at other times thrills them with its versatility. Use the definition in your anthology or the one that follows.

Definition: "Poetry is literature designed to *convey* a vivid and imaginative sense of experience, especially by the use of *condensed* language *chosen* for its sound and *suggestive* power as well as for its meaning and by the use of such literary devices as *structured* meter, *natural cadences*, rhyme, and metaphor."[2]

Read the definition aloud a couple of times, letting your voice emphasize the italicized words. Then dictate it slowly so students can write the definition in their journals. Afterward, project the definition so they can verify their writing.

Why this laborious start? Hearing, listening, writing, and viewing are ways to reinforce the concept. This definition will form the basis of subsequent reflections on the form and function of poetry studied throughout the unit. Having a definition of a specific kind of writing aids close reading and deeper understanding of the genre as well as how to make sense of it as students experiment with writing it.

Take a few moments more and ask students what they think the italicized words mean in the context of poetry. If no one offers definitions, direct them to locate the words in a print or digital dictionary and to share the definitions with the class.

This is a situation when it is good to have stored dictionaries under students' desks or on shelves around the room so they can reach them easily without having to ask or disrupt others. It should not be unusual to see one or more of them reaching for a dictionary during any class meeting. Encourage students to add a dictionary link right on their tablet or cellphone landing page. They will find it handy during this unit of study.

Now return to the poem "Unfolding Bud" or "My Poems Have Holes Sewn into Them" and again ask the class what they imagine either poem is saying to them about reading poetry. What elements of the definition have Koriyama and/or Troupe used in their poems?

To solidify understanding, end the lesson by having students read aloud in unison the definition of poetry they have written in their notebooks, and then, like a Greek chorus, read one of the opening poems. The left side of the class can read stanza one; the right side, stanza two, and in unison, the whole class can read stanza three.

SWIMMING AROUND IN POEMS

For homework, you can assign students to peruse their literature anthology or other poetry collections they have, can borrow, find in the library or online. Ask them to read and list four or five poems, and then handwrite into their notebook at least one poem they particularly like. If such an out-of-class assignment is not a realistic expectation for the students you have, during the next class meeting, allot in-class time for them to look through their anthology or the poetry books you have collected for their use in the classroom.

Ask each student to select and copy into his or her own notebook one or two poems that attract their attention. For those using computers, have them key in the poem rather than simply copying and pasting. The physical act of handwriting or keying in the poem slows them down a bit so they can pay attention to (1) individual words, (2) line structure, and (3) patterns in poetry—three distinguishing features of this genre of literature.

Your students then have a self-selected poem to refer to and share with the class later during the unit. The value of this assignment is that it gives them an opportunity to read a variety of poems for which they are not required to do anything more than choose one they like. And the bonus? They are likely to read twice as many poems this way than if you were to assign a specific one to read for class. The next class meeting simply record in the grade book whether or not each student has the poem. The goal here is to get them reading poetry and to become more at ease with this literary form.

USING POPULAR SONG LYRICS TO INTRODUCE POETRY

Encourage students to bring in song lyrics that are appropriate for sharing in class. Until you point it out, probably few adolescents recognize that song lyrics often are poems. Having them bring in song lyrics and poems of their choice also is a way for you to become more familiar with what current teens listen to and find interesting. They also feel as though they are a part of the learning process because they are helping shape the lessons. Depending on the students you teach, you may wish to collect and read the lyrics first, then use them for a lesson later in the unit.

INTRODUCING POETRY T.I.M.E: A STRATEGY FOR POETRY ANALYSIS

Poetry T.I.M.E has been around for decades. This idea for poetry analysis has been passed along from teacher to teacher across the nation. You, too, may have been taught this way and find this clever acronym just what you need to organize your instruction and enhance student learning. If you choose to use it, you are likely to have former students return to express their appreciation for having a mnemonic that serves them well on standardized and placement tests as well as on final exams in other courses. In relation to poetry, T.I.M.E. stands for (1) title, thought, and theme, (2) imagery, (3) music, and (4) emotion, expressed by the author and experienced by the reader/listener. (See figure 6.1.)

120   *Chapter 6*

Knowing this acronym can help students unlock meaning in poetry. As they have learned in their readings of the Koriyama and Troupe selections, poems are written in condensed language and often require multiple readings. T.I.M.E. really is a pun and refers not only to the fact that it often takes more time to read and write poetry, but also refers to elements of a poem that, when considered independently, can lead to a deeper understanding of the poem in its entirety. Taking T.I.M.E. for poetry will help them recognize the holes poets like Quincy Troupe may have conscientiously or unconsciously sewn into their poems.

"T" Stands for Title, Thought, Theme

Begin with "T," for the title of a poem. If a poet has chosen a title, it often serves as a hint to what the poem is about and may indicate the emotion or opinion the poet has about the experience related in the poem. The title may be a peephole into the interior the reader will explore once inside the poem. The "T" could also stand for the thought or theme of the poem. This is a flexible acronym, and you can decide the best word(s) to use with the students you have. You may use one, two, or three of these "T" words. All are related to the study of poetry.

Figure 6.1 (Illustration by Nabeel Usmani)

Just for fun, project a copy of the poem "Finalists," by Nancy Genevieve. Do not show the students the title when you ask them what the poem is about. Then show them the title and ask how their understanding of the poem changes. Ask them to look at the poem they have written in their journals. How might the message be changed if there was no title?

>   "Finalists"
>   Seven turkey vultures
>   on the uppermost gable
>   of the cow barn
>   Preening.[2]

Next, draw the students' attention to concepts about the speaker and audience. Published poetry is meant to be understood. You may choose to clarify this idea and specify "published poetry" because many people write poetry just for themselves and may not care whether anyone else even reads it let alone understands it. Generally, though, a poet is someone saying something to someone. That first someone is "the speaker" who may or may not be the poet.

For example, you may have a poet, an elderly woman who writes a poem in the persona of an adolescent boy. In this situation, though the poet is a woman, the speaker in the poem is a boy. Looking at the kind of pronouns used, the vocabulary and images can help the reader imagine the audience. One visual way that helps students think of poetry as a piece of writing with a message is to use a graphic design, as shown in figure 6.2, with three spaces—one large rectangle in the middle of the page and small circle on the left and a larger one on right of the large rectangle.

After they make this full-page chart in the poetry section of their journals, ask your students to draw a picture of a possible speaker in the small circle on the left and in the large circle on the right, a possible audience: one

POETRY IS

SOMEONE saying SOMETHING to *SOMEONE(s)

*a specific individual, kind of person, group of people

Figure 6.2

person, a special person, or a group of people, all within the large circle. Then, in the rectangle in the center, write a sentence summary of what the poem could be saying and quote a couple lines from the poem to support their opinion.

Demonstrate how this could work by referring first to "My Poems Have Holes Sewn into Them" by Quincy Troupe and then to "Unfolding Bud" by Naoshi Koriyama. Draw the graphic organizer on the board and then ask students, "Who could be the speaker?" "Who could be the audience?" For the Koriyama poem, typical answers include a parent talking to a student who is doing his or her homework and persuades the young person to hang in there and not give up just because the poem is difficult to understand after one or two readings. Some may respond that it is a teacher speaking to an individual student or the class as a whole.

To reinforce the ideas of speaker and audience, distribute a copy of Emily Dickinson's poem "I'm Nobody." Ask the students to read it and think of as many different speaker and audience sets as they can. Ask them to imagine this poem was to be spoken by a character in a play or movie. What could be the setting? Who could be the speaker? Who could be the audience? The only limitation is that the sets must be supported by the words of the poem. Your students may come up with combinations or settings such as

- a student new to the school talking to another student at lunch time
- a new player on an athletic team to another player
- a prisoner talking to another prisoner
- a new teacher at the first department meeting
- a boy at the playground during a pick up soccer, football, or basketball game
- a rock singer waiting to perform on a TV program
- a girl at a skateboarding competition
- an actress trying out for a part in a play to another actress
- a parent talking to another parent during the school open house
- a woman attending a neighborhood luncheon for the first time

If you are in the mood, act a little silly, ham it up and reread the poem in the voices and persona of the pairs students suggest. Great fun! Makes the point, too, of multiple possibilities but common meanings.

"I" Stands for the Imagery in Poetry

Poets use words to help create pictures, emotions, or memories of incidents in the minds of readers and listeners, using sensory or figurative images or a combination of the two. Sensory imagery, you recall, appeals to one or more

**TITLE
THOUGHT(S)
THEME(S)**

"T" of T.I.M.E.

(Illustration by Nabeel Usmani)

of the five senses: sight, hearing, taste, touch, and smell. It is through our senses that we experience the world, and many poets appeal to them as they re-create their own experiences in poetic form.

Rather than presenting this portion of the lesson as lecture, simply draw or project an eye, an ear, a mouth, a hand, and a nose on the board. Then, ask the students to label the drawings and give examples of words or phrases that appeal to the senses. Prepare for the lesson by looking at a variety of poems, compiling sample lines from poems that illustrate appeals to the various senses. Better yet, invite students to offer lines they recall from familiar song lyrics, but be prepared with your examples just to prime the pump, to get them thinking.

This would be a good time to ask students to look back at the poems they selected and copied into their journals at the beginning of the unit. Set your timer for five minutes and have them look at the poem and mark images. Then, reset for ten minutes, have them pull their desks together, or turn to a table partner and then share with a partner these poems, pointing out examples of sensory images from their chosen poems.

(Illustration by Nabeel Usmani)

Working with poems they have chosen validates the assignment to choose and copy them into their notebooks. Invite volunteers to read aloud to the class lines that illustrate the sensory images they find. Variety spices the lessons and increases interest.

Next, direct their attention to figurative imagery. Many middle school students have learned about similes and metaphors in earlier grades and are able to define them for the class. Some know "personification"; fewer know "hyperbole" and "symbol" and "allusion." Be prepared to introduce these devices and give students definitions and examples. Here are some simple definitions of these types of figurative imagery:

- *Simile*: a comparison between two things using "like" or "as." Example: The thunder roared like a bear.
- *Metaphor*: an implied comparison between two things without using the words "like" or "as." Example: Dime-sized raindrops pelted me in the face.
- *Hyperbole*: exaggeration to create an effect. Example: That goldfish is as big as my leg!

- *Personification*: giving a nonhuman thing the characteristics of a person. Example: The dog smirked and snatched up my sandwich.

Occasionally a poet uses a *symbol*—something concrete that stands for something else: an abstract concept, another thing, idea, or event. For example, a "flag" is a cloth on a stick. But a certain configuration of colors and shapes such as stars on a blue rectangular field in the upper-left corner of a red- and white-striped cloth suggests the American flag, which stands for the nation, freedom, and patriotism.

Symbols can be a great opening to talk about cultural contexts, too. For example, a snake or serpent symbolizes different ideas depending on the culture, the religion, or the nation. Red in some cultures is a sad color representing blood or anger; in other cultures, it is a happy color representing marriage or royalty.

An *allusion* is a reference to another body of literature, a movie, or an incident the writer believes the readers know. Allusions can help the writer create an image with just a few words because the writer believes the allusion automatically triggers memories, ideas, or emotions from its reference in the poem. Your students may enjoy playing with this poetic device in much the same way Nancy Genevieve has in these few lines from her poem "A Kiss":

> Enchanted innocent kissed the frog
> and heard only a croak in reply.
> Will you, child, kiss it again
> and give him another try?
> Or will you release him
> and then begin to cry?
> Or worse, will you never ever
> give another frog a chance?[3]

In Western literature, allusions frequently are made to *The Holy Bible* with its Hebrew and Christian Scriptures; Roman and Greek mythology; Shakespeare's writings; and fairy tales. Sometimes a reference may be made to familiar movie like *Star Trek* or *Black Panther*, or a historical incident like the Civil War or the Gold Rush. If your students represent a range of cultures and national origins, select samples from the literature and historical events that are more familiar to them. Consider stories, myths, and sacred texts they may know from literature and life in Central and South America, Asia, Africa, and Australia.

You could spend the remainder of the period looking at examples of poems that have strong imagery. Project copies of two poems already discussed as a class. Then ask students to find examples of all kinds of imagery to share and compare with a partner, and encourage them to copy favorite

Poets re-create experience with words that create images

lines into their journals. Remember, in order to find their own examples, students read much more poetry than if you provide all the examples. Equally important is the fact that each year you teach the unit you are learning and discovering the kinds of poems that interest students in each different class.

Students enjoy pointing out figurative language in the poems that follow. Notice the ways that Nancy Genevieve uses metaphors and personification in her poems "Evening Cicadas."

> Evening cicadas
>   tune up for night
>   practicing their
>   lull-a-bye for summer.[4]

This short poem illustrates so well the personification that can bring such a personal appeal to a poem. What images do your students notice in this next one "The Pond"?

> Bubbles frozen in ice
> Pearls of silence
> waiting for spring.

> Crystals etched in glaze
> Petals of illusion,
> blooming by night.
> Twilight bathed in mist
> flames of fading,
> seeping into no more.

Patterning Poetry: Teacher and Student Responses

An assignment that always evokes positive responses and pretty good poetry is one on patterning poems. Ask students to select one or two of the poems that they particularly like either from their anthology or one of the books in your room. Next ask them to think of a memorable experience of their own. Finally, invite them to pattern the structure and imagery of one of their chosen poems to re-create the experience of that incident. Of course, if you are writing poems along with them (and you should), you experience how it feels like to write on demand as you are asking them to do. Then you, too, have something newly written to read during sharing time.

For example, you could ask your students to write lyric poem like Robert Frost's "Acquainted with the Night," or a short piece that patterns a ballad, like "Barbara Allen." Here's a ballad I wrote with my students patterned like that one:

> Oh, it was around Christmas time
> When the marriage, it was planned.
> The family and friends all came to see
> Sir William wed Lady Ann.
>
> The musicians were seated, all playing their songs
> Awaiting the groom to appear.
> And seated among the guests that day
> Sat his former love, Lady Mear.
>
> The minister signaled the groom to come out
> To stand with best man at the right.
> The minister motioned the guests to stand
> As the bride marched in dressed in white.
>
> Lady Mear, she stood with hankie in hand
> Weeping for the man she had lost.
> She'd been too proud to accept the ring
> Sir William had gotten at cost.

The bride advanced at a stately pace
By her handsome groom to stand
Lady Mear, near the aisle, could be heard for a mile,
Shouting, "Hey Lady Ann, that's my man!"

Sir William's response to the lady's outburst,
"You had my heart in your hand.
You cast me aside. Yes, I did love you first,
But today, I'll wed Lady Ann."

So that day long ago about Christmas time,
The guests got more than was planned.
An old love turned mean in quite a wild scene
When Sir William wed Lady Ann.

—Anna J. Small Roseboro aka Mrs. William
G. Roseboro, "The Ballad of William and Ann"
patterned after "Barbara Allen" Anonymous Poet

"M" Stands for Music: The Sound of Poetry

According to the definition used earlier, poets choose words "for their sound and suggestive power." Now let's look at three aspects of music and poetry: (1) rhythm, (2) rhyme, and (3) the sound of words. Some poets

"M" of T.I.M.E.

(Illustration by Nabeel Usmani)

arrange their words to create a pattern of beats or *rhythm*. If your students are ready, teach the I.T.A.D.S., an acronym for five common poetic rhythm patterns—iambic, trochaic, anapestic, dactylic, and spondee. These words identify the patterns of stressed and unstressed syllables, information students surely are expected to know and use in high school and beyond.

During this lesson on music, mention to the students that I.T.A.D.S patterns are called the "feet" of poetry. There is only one stressed syllable in each foot. Explain that a poem's rhythm, or the "meter," is named for the number of feet or beats per line and the kind of foot that is in each line.

For example, a line of poetry with four feet or four beats is tetrameter (*tetra* is Greek for four). If the feet are iambic—one unstressed syllable followed by a stressed one—the line is identified as iambic tetrameter. Have fun by asking students to identify the rhythm patterns of their own names. Anna is trochaic. Jamar is iambic. Small is spondee. Roseboro is dactylic. What are the patterns of your name?

Moving to the Music of Poetry

Because many students are kinesthetic learners and can remember what they feel physically, you should demonstrate the rhythms of poetry that way, too. Read a poem with a strong beat while students are standing up and marching in place. How about inviting them to clap their hands, tap one foot, or snap their fingers to the beat?

To use that abundance of energy, have the students march around the room when you read William Wordsworth's "Daffodils": "I wander'd lonely as a cloud." Rather than wandering quietly, stomp loudly. Use your arms to sway broadly from side to side to show the rhythm of the waves in John Masefield's "Sea Fever": "I *must* go down to the seas again, to the *lonely* sea and the sky." Of course, they see right away the rhythm of song lyrics, but you could save this until later. For now, acknowledge that "just as some poetry has a specific rhythm pattern, so do the lyrics or words of some songs you know."

Listening for Patterns of Sounds

A second way to look at the music of poetry is to consider the *rhyme*, which occurs when words with similar sounds are used in an observable pattern. The rhyme may occur at the end of a line or within a line.

Students can discover the pattern of rhyme by using letters of the alphabet to indicate repeated sounds. For example, begin writing with the letter "a" at the end of the first line of poetry. If the second line ends with the same sound, write "a" again. If it ends with a different sound, change to "b." Continue throughout the poem to determine if there is a pattern and what the pattern is.

The narrative poem "The Cremation of Sam McGee" by Robert W. Service makes particularly interesting reading when you are teaching internal and end rhyme. The macabre story is intriguing, too. Check out the online versions in which Robert Service and Johnny Cash each have recorded their renditions of this narrative poem. Your students may enjoy the photos, too.

Point out that free and blank verse poetry have no systematic rhyme pattern. You probably plan to discuss this kind of poetry later in your unit, but should mention it out now, particularly if students bring in examples of free-verse poetry or notice it in their class anthology. This is why it is good to begin the unit with the definition of poetry that mentions structured meter or natural cadences. Your discussion of the music of poetry gives space to talk about blank and free verse without having to provide another definition or having to back pedal when they point out that some poetry is unstructured in terms of rhythm and rhyme.

Seeing Song Lyrics as Poetry

Now is an optimal time to ask selected students to read aloud lyrics of their favorite songs. Most have a steady beat and many rhymes, making more concrete the connection between poetry of music and poetry in books easier to comprehend. Be prepared for students to show more interest in what they bring to the class.

Show your enthusiasm as you look at and listen to what they bring. They are providing you a window into their worlds, and what you learn reveals what they know and indicates what you may need to teach or reteach as you continue planning learning experiences for your poetry unit. Combine the familiar with the new by encouraging your students to use the vocabulary of poetry as they talk about song lyrics they choose themselves.

If you have the nerve of most middle school teachers, you can "prove" the link between poetry and music by singing the "I'm Nobody" poem to either "Yellow Rose of Texas" or "America, the Beautiful"! Even if you are a very good singer, the students probably are going to laugh at you, but they also remember the lesson. Is that not the goal of teaching?

Sensory Image of Sounds

A third way to talk about the music or sound of poetry is to point out *onomatopoeia*, words that are spelled to imitate the sound they describe. Teens love making peculiar, sometimes-shocking and vulgar noises. One way to exploit that particular pleasure is to have the students write poems that capture the sounds of everyday experiences. A seventh grader wrote "The Kitchen" about the sounds at home. Like Shakespeare, this student enjoys making up words, too.

> With a cling clang
> Not a bang or dang
> a swish and a wish
> all the dishes are in the sink
> screech creach
> open
> close
> scuffles ruffles
> a sea of bubbles and water
> a crounging rounging
> with a turn of the knob
> all the dishes are clean
> then click click click
> whoosh.
> Are you hungry for lunch yet?

Another way to address sound as you discuss the music of poetry is to consider repetition of vowels (*assonance*) or consonants (*consonance* or *alliteration*). Most students recognize tongue twisters as examples of alliteration.

Emotional Power of Sounds

Students are intrigued to learn that the sound of words suggests certain emotions, too. For example, a poet who wishes to convey the emotion or sense of experience in a calm, peaceful way is likely to select soft-sounding consonants like l, m, n, and s. If the memory is unpleasant or bitter, the poet is likely to pick hard consonants that must be forced through the lips and teeth to be formed, like p, t, f, or guttural sounds like k, g, and j. A graphic way to illustrate this can be pointing out that most obscene words in English include these harsh, guttural, and dental sounds.

Of course, you need not say them aloud or write them down. Students know the words if you refer to "the F word" or "the S word." They smile and smirk, and your point is made. If many of your students speak other languages, and if you can maintain control of the class, you may ask them if profane words in their language follow this pattern of harsh sounds. Again, let them think, but not speak the words. The point is made.

"E" of T.I.M.E.

(Illustration by Nabeel Usmani)

Letter "E" Stands for Emotions

The emotion expressed by the poet and the emotion experienced by the reader may very well be different. How do students discover these emotions? By paying attention to the kinds of images (comparisons to positive or negative things), and the music, rhyme, rhythm, and sounds of words the poet uses to convey the experience of the poem.

The students may find examples of emotions expressed such as pride, love, grief/distress, fear, joy, jealousy, or shame/embarrassment. They may experience similar feelings as they read or hear the poems, but the emotion expressed and experienced often is not the same! Have them try their new analyzing skills reading and talking about "The Boy in the Window" by Richard Wilbur.

If the students are ready, teach them that the "tone" of a poem refers to the author's attitude or feeling about the topic or experience related in the poem. On the other hand, "mood" refers to the way the poem makes the reader feel when he or she reads or hears a poem. To help make the link more personal, you can draw their attention to the M in mood and say, "Mood means the way the poem makes ME, the reader, feel." That usually is sufficient instruction at this time. As you teach these poetry terms, continue to encourage students to use them regularly when talking and writing about poetry. Such use raises the level of their conversation and expands their working vocabulary. Makes them feel oh so sophisticated!

SPENDING T.I.M.E. READING POEMS INDEPENDENTLY

One way for students to practice reading on their own without feeling undue pressure is to ask them to continue bringing in poems and to point out the ways their self-selected poems reflect the various elements already studied. This subtly entices them to read more widely. They are likely to return to the books skimmed before and come across poems that speak to them differently this time.

Giving this assignment again also reveals to you how students' choice of poetry is being modified by the series of lessons you are teaching. Invite them to post their choices on your class website, remembering to include the title, author, and source. Or, they can print out copies and staple those on a bulletin board set aside for this purpose in your classroom and labeled "Poems We Like."

As they seek out poems, encourage your students to interview their family members to learn about their favorite poems. It's surprising how amazed teens are to learn that their moms, dads, aunts, uncles, and even grandparents had to memorize and recite poetry as regular part of their literature coursework! If they speak languages other than English at home, invite them to bring in poems by favorite poets in those languages and read them aloud to the class. This affirms their heritage and expands the cultural experience for you and their classmates as well.

Allow plenty of class time for students to immerse themselves in the poetry you have assembled in the classroom, their anthology, and the websites you recommend or have posted on your website. Those who have not done so before may now choose to bring in lyrics from their favorite songs—appropriate ones, of course! Consider including an assignment to recite a suitable poem of their choice. For sample lessons, see companion website at http://teachingenglishlanguagearts.com.

You know to alert your students to the fact that poems address an array of topics in a variety of ways. Remind your eager young teens to use their judgment on which poems would be appropriate to share in class. Thankfully, by this time in the course or school year, you have established a classroom milieu for sensitive reading and sensible selections. However, reminding them at this time is still a good idea.

> ### Questions to Ask about Poetry
> 1. What does the title suggest about the poem?
> 2. Who could be the speaker? Indicate clues in the text to support this supposition.
> 3. Who could be the audience? Indicate clues in the text to support this supposition.
> 4. What literary devices/techniques has the poet used?
> 5. How do these elements work to create the total impact on me? (mood)
> 6. What do you think the poet feels about the topic of this poem? (tone)
> 7. What do I imagine is a message or theme of the poem?
> 8. What clues in the text support this the message or the theme?

Figure 6.3 Questions like these help unlock poems

Notice in figure 6.3 the use of "a message or theme" is to keep the poem open for students to draw from it what the poem says to them. As soon as you suggest the "meaning," they begin guessing and hoping they come up with the "right" answer. With self-control, you can let the poems speak for themselves.

As you plan to teach poetry in a more formal way, schedule time to assign an extensive poetry project such as those described in the "Language Arts Resources" section on the companion website for this book. There are two outlines for poetry units in which students collect and share poems they find and ones they write. Both poetry units require them to write original poems as a way to practice the various poetic devices you study.

ASSIGNING THE POETRY PROJECT OR NOTEBOOK

An effective way to reinforce the interests raised and skills developed during a poetry unit is to have students assemble a poetry notebook. The collection should include poems they have read and enjoyed as well as poems they have written themselves. Decide how much time you have to devote to this project and select activities that may be organized around one or more of the following topics:

- poems by a single poet
- poems written on a single theme (love, family, hobby, seasons, etc.)
- poems employing common poetic devices
- poems reflecting a specific culture or nationality

T.I.M.E. MNEMONIC

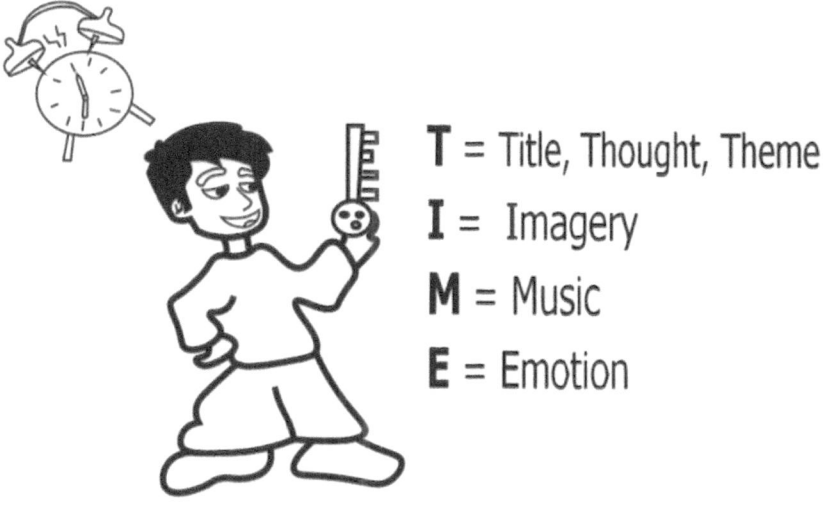

T.I.M.E. is key to understanding poetry (Illustration by Nabeel Usmani)

It is imperative to inform your students at the beginning of the poetry unit that they are to create for this poetry notebook. In this way they can think about and collect poems throughout the weeks you spend on formal poetry study.

CONCLUSION

Few readers deny either that poets tend to write cryptically or that it takes more effort to discover what poets have to say to their listeners and readers. When you teach your students to tell the T.I.M.E. of a poem, you give your adolescent readers a golden key they can use for life. Using this key, they know to look systematically for different aspects of the poem on each reread. They experience delight of discovery and enthusiasm of empowerment when you give them T.I.M.E. to study this genre of literature. As when traveling in a new country, sampling new and different foods, students may even develop gustatory joy from sampling this genre of literary expression. Through the guided practice you offer, even squirmy adolescents slow down and pay attention to the words, layouts, forms, sounds, and eventually to messages in poetry. They may even astonish you when their careful reading leads to interpretations like those that published critics write about the poems!

By the end of your formal instruction along this school year journey, your students feel far more confident about studying this challenging literary genre. They may not have the ease of Huck Finn's friend Emmeline Grangerford and be able to "slap down a line . . . just scratch it out and slap down another one,"[6] but they now are able to read, write, and talk more confidently about poetry in their own way. Your young teens can respond to those "prodigiously stirring words" and feel comfortable putting pen to paper to capture the "viscerally urging words" that become poems of their own.

NOTES

1. Quincy Troupe, "My Poems Have Holes Sewn Into Them." In *Transcircularities: New and Selected poems*, ed. Quincy Troupe, 98–99, 1st edition. (Minneapolis, MN: Coffee House Press, 2002).

2. *Houghton-Mifflin College Dictionary*, 1986, s.v. "poetry."

3. Nancy Genevieve, "Finalists." In *American Religion and Literature Society Newsletter*, ed. Deshae Lott (Spring 2007).

4. Nancy Genevieve, "The Pond" and "Cicadas." In *NYX: Daughter of Chaos*, (Temple Terrace, FL: NOX Press, 2002).

5. Nancy Genevieve, "A Kiss." In *NYX: Mother of Light*, NYX Series, vol. 2 (Temple Terrace, FL: NOX Press, 2001) and *ELM* 5, no. 2 (Spring 1997).

6. "If Emmeline Grangerford could make poetry like that before she was fourteen, there ain't no telling what she could a done by-and-by. Buck said she could rattle off poetry like nothing. She didn't ever have to stop to think. He said she would slap down a line, and if she couldn't find anything to rhyme with it she would just scratch it out and slap down another one, and go ahead." From page 7 in chapter 17 of *The Adventures of Huckleberry Finn* by Mark Twain. https://www.shmoop.com/huckleberry-finn/chapter-17-full-text-7.html (accessed October 11, 2018).

Chapter 7

Playing It Right: Reading and Writing about Drama

> I order you to be silent! And I issue a collective challenge! Come, I'll write down your names. Step forward, young heroes! You'll all have a turn; I'll give each of you a number. Now, who wants to be at the top of the list? You, sir? No? You? No? [Silence] No names? No hands. . . . Then I'll get on with my business.[1]
>
> —Cyrano speaking in *Cyrano de Bergerac,* by Edmond Rostand

Cyrano's rousing speech may not have been as successful as he would have liked, but he certainly delivered it with enthusiasm and passion. You need the same passion to draw your students into reading with joy and understanding drama. In this chapter are techniques that can produce a far better response than poor Cyrano elicited.

Drama permeates teachers' and students' lives via TV, movies, school productions, YouTube, and so many other venues. This pervasiveness makes it a challenge to teach dramatic literature simply by reading it or writing drama without reading it. But that is just the way some drama is handled in the typical English classes. That need not be the case with you.

Your students need to stretch their dramatic creativity, imagining what words could sound like spoken on stage and what characters and scenes could look like on stage. Teaching a work of drama is a superb opportunity to broaden their experience with literature and to expand their understanding of the unique features of this literary genre. This chapter describes ways to help students further develop their own expressive and oral reading skills.

Here are ideas from lessons on *Cyrano de Bergerac* for seventh graders, *Romeo and Juliet* for eighth or ninth graders. Even if you teach older students, you can adapt these ideas for your setting. See the companion website

You can get organized and have a great time

Allow time for students to work out scenes

for other ideas of plays to consider teaching in addition to or in place of what already is in your curriculum.[2]

Drama, like other narrative literature, is written to tell a story of characters facing conflict. In this genre, dramatists create their narratives to be performed by actors who assume the roles of characters in the story. In drama, however, the setting—the time and place—is revealed primarily through sets, lights, props, and costumes, and readers must rely more heavily on the dialogue that reveals character and advances plot.[3]

Unfortunately, inexperienced students are tempted to skip those important stage directions; these readers tend to jump directly to the dialogue. Then they become confused, even frustrated when they do not understand what is really happening. Consequently, the aspects of drama to teach first are its unique features, pointing out those distinctive elements as you remind your maturing readers that characters and conflict are common to fiction in general.

PLANNING AHEAD

Plan your assignments so students can read aloud each day and so all who want to have an opportunity to read one major role at least once. If they can be depended upon to study the scenes ahead of time at home, assign parts as homework so students can practice reading aloud. Otherwise, allow class time for silent reading so they can be familiar with the lines and able to read them expressively in character. Few things dampen enthusiasm for studying drama more than poor oral reading. To interpret the roles effectively, your young actors need to know what is going on and what the lines portend.

Keep in mind, too, that plays are written to be viewed in a single theatrical sitting (perhaps with intermissions). Therefore, if you stretch out the initial reading over too many days or weeks, you lose the essence of the drama—so keep the action alive. Once the class has read the exposition of the play and students are familiar with the main characters and the problem(s) to be solved, move as quickly through the play as possible. Then after you have read the entire play, go back and have them practice and present scenes, and talk about the effectiveness of the literary devices the dramatist has used to create in this genre.

This doubling back reinforces and clarifies what may have been missed on the original reading. Even as skillful a reader as you are, you are not likely to have come to the level of understanding you have on just a single read of the play. To enhance conversations and enrich discussion, assume a complete first reading is needed and allot time for rereading and time for small groups to perform selected scenes. Include drafting a one-act play in your unit and, once the students begin writing their own original scenes, allot time for reading aloud their drafts to help ensure their final scripts sound more like real dialogue.

It's good to get the students up and moving

As students begin working in groups to make decisions on how to act out the play, anticipate the four natural stages of development: forming, storming, norming, and performing. Be prepared for them to grumble that their part is too large or too small; encourage them to decide on staging that includes simple costumes and/or props; consider naming as the director "whoever is creating the biggest stink!" Most of all, keep in mind while students prepare to present scenes that the best-laid plans often are better modified than forced.

The keys for success are to have a goal, explain it, and then let students plan how to implement it. However, they still need you there. Be observant; step in firmly so they use more class time practicing than bickering. Setting your timer to ring ten minutes before the period ends helps. Then use these final ten minutes to rearrange the room, reflect on what went well, and remind them of the next day's assignment. The sooner they begin planning and practicing, the more likely your young thespians are to learn and enjoy drama. Oh yes, this is a noisy activity!

Attending Live Performances

Check to see if a local theater company is scheduled to perform the play your students are to study. If so, try to attend it. Preparing to see the performance provides another occasion to talk about the difference between

Experiencing live theater enhances study of drama as genre

reading a play and seeing it performed. Even if it is not convenient to take a whole class to a play, you may be able to invite members of the cast to visit your school. If a play appropriate for young adults is being staged, but different from what you plan to teach, still consider taking your students to see it. Experiencing a good live theater performance enhances your teaching and extends their learning.

Many community theater groups have educational outreach programs established to introduce young people to live theater. You may have local performers who would count it a privilege to come to your school and talk about their profession with students. You may even find a live performance in another version for them to see, such as a ballet or an operatic staging of *Romeo and Juliet*. If you begin planning early enough, you should be able to coordinate your lesson planning with one such scheduled local production.

What if performance prices are high or your school is not near a college or civic theater program that may offer lower rates? Ask around. Consider local community theater groups. Put out the word that you are looking for someone in the area with stage experience; you might find a terrific and inexpensive guest speaker thrilled to come. Also, investigate organizations that might help underwrite the cost of bringing in a touring group; service organizations like the Kiwanis, Rotary, Lions, and Optimist Clubs; local foundations and arts associations are possibilities, too.

Planning the Field Trip

If you are new to your school or district and you decide to plan an outing to the theater, consult with your administrator and seek advice from other teachers who have experience with field trips. Trips can take weeks of planning: coming up with the finances; raising the funds for those who cannot afford tickets; transportation, chaperones, and permission slips. Do not be dissuaded by naysayers. Attending a live performance can be an eye-opening experience well worth the effort you expend. Careful planning can make it a pleasure.

Young students enjoy being known as a respectful audience. You can help them become one. You see, ushers at school-age performances of plays held at local theaters know which schools and which teachers at those schools have well-mannered groups. You can inspire commendable behavior even in rowdy young teenagers. Believe it or not, what they wear makes a difference, but no need to tell them how important it may be to you. Instead, urge students to dress for the occasion with special attire appropriate for your community. When teenagers are dressed well, they seem to behave better.

The public talks, so do what you can to prepare your students to confirm your school's good reputation or to surprise others that your class is better behaved than expected. For some this may be their first experience with live theater. It is exciting for them. Some will be awed by the ambience. You can allay their anxiety and reduce their squirrely behavior if you can show them pictures of the interior and a layout of the facility. This will increase their curiosity and prepare them for what to expect.

Encourage them to talk about the experience before, during the ride to and from the theater, and afterward in the classroom. For some students, this entire process may be a highlight of the school year. They may even decide to write a play about their going to see one!

LITERARY DEVICES AND VOCABULARY IN DRAMA

Studying a play with your students is an excellent opportunity to expand or reinforce the list of literary terms you taught when they were reading short fiction, novels and poetry. For example, as you study *Cyrano de Bergerac*, this list could include those elements that Rostand used so brilliantly, such as:

- allusion
- ballad
- dramatic irony
- mood
- verbal irony

If the play is in your anthology, you may rely on the literary terms and vocabulary featured in the text. The editorial staff usually does a fine job of selecting words students using that text need to know to understand the play, along with some that would be good for them to add to their speaking and writing vocabularies.

Of course, take time for students to look up and talk about any other words that interest them or trip them up when they are reading or discussing the play you have chosen. By the second semester when many course outlines suggest teaching drama, the students are comfortable with each other and with you and are open to acknowledging gaps in their understanding, and accustomed to looking up words they do not know.

GETTING INTO READING THE PLAY

The best preparation for attending an off-site performance is a good in-class experience with a play. Start with the list of characters, the author's description of setting, and the stage directions. Encourage students to predict. For example, if characters are family members, ask them what conflicts they anticipate among those persons considering their age and gender. Think about the setting. What is likely to occur in the time and place the author has chosen? Based on the stage directions, where should the characters be positioned when the curtain opens?

If students previously have studied the elements of fiction, they may anticipate from these opening observations and even predict that the play will follow the now-familiar plot line with exposition, rising action, climax, falling action, and resolution.

Establishing Visual Historical Context for a Play

Dramatic scripts tell the readers as well as the director when and where the action takes place. If the time and place are unfamiliar to students, show them photos or video clips to help them visualize the setting as they read the dialogue. Websites like YouTube and Vimeo, along with video archive sites sponsored by the American Film Institute and the UCLA film archives, provide tens of thousands of short clips that:

- were shot in historical location,
- re-create historical settings and locations, and
- illustrate both costuming and dialogue for historical periods.

These sites are not always easily searchable by keyword, so it's best to search concretely by the names of films that you have already linked to a period. Preview everything.

Staging Tableaux

To help students get a feel for drama, ask them to read the opening scene silently. Then, with no explanation from you of what they have read, invite one student to come silently to the front of the class and stand where a specific character would stand if he or she were on stage. Then, beckon other students, one at a time, to assume the persona of the another character and take their places in relation to those already positioned in the front. Ask the rest of the class to observe silently until all of the scene's characters are positioned. At that time, call for a freeze to create a tableau, montage, or representation of that scene.

Now ask the class its opinions of the character placement. Before those in the tableau lose their concentration and begin squirming or melting, unfreeze them so they can return to their seats to join the discussion. Invite participants from the tableau to identify lines from the play that support their own choice of position. Others can look at the text of the play to determine passages that justify the tableau just presented or to propose an arrangement more accurate to the text.

Of course, those who disagree should be asked to quote from the text to show why an alternate placement seems more accurate. Taking time to consider placement on the stage will help your students write more realistic drama when they begin their own scripts.

JOURNALING SETS THE STAGE FOR UNDERSTANDING

Your well-taught students know to pay attention to what happens in the opening sections of any work of fiction whether short story, narrative poetry, or novel. As they continue reading the play on their own, they are able to follow the plot line, and to answer in their journals such questions as

- Who are the protagonist and antagonist(s)?
- What is the conflict?
- When does the main action occur?
- Where does the main action take place (other than on stage)?
- Why do characters act the way they do?
- How does the writer have the characters solve the problems raised in the play?

Assigning this writing activity about the opening act focuses students' attention on the main characters as they are being introduced, as well as the conflicts that play writers reveal early in the exposition of their works. Yes, the script lists the names in the cast of characters; some dramatists even mention the relationship among the characters, but the reader/viewer usually does not know the personality or motivations of these characters until the play begins. Since you want your students to be able to follow the play without having to go back too often to figure out who's who and what's what, assign this five Ws and H journal entry right away.

INTENTIONAL SLOW STARTS SPEED UP READING

Begin the play slowly enough for your students to get a firm handle on these relationships; it makes the rest of the reading go more smoothly. Then you can spend your time inviting students to read aloud, in character, and to discuss their understanding of the plot while paying attention to character development, plot advancement, and theme revelation. But don't get bogged down in analytical mud. Students do not have enough insight yet to hold meaningful discussions about structure and still are trying to figure out what happens next. Save those analytical conversations for the reread.

Now, after closely reading Act I, trust the author to show what is going on among the characters so the audience can understand the personalities and conflicts themselves. This approach to quick reading is in keeping with the idea that plays are written to be viewed in one sitting or at least a single theater visit.

As when beginning other works of fiction, during the first few days of reading a play, remind students to mark their texts, use their sticky notes, or record in their journals the words or phrases that reveal specific facts about characters, especially motivation. By this time, most of them already are active readers so there is no need to plod through the entire play, stopping to identify this basic information but answer questions as they arise.

Taking Notes While Reading

While a quick read is usually best for overall narrative comprehension, many film-oriented students have difficulty tracking characters because they cannot see them. They may benefit from a simple graphic organizer. If your students are not permitted to write in their books, assign them to keep character-related notes in their reading journal. They can make three columns:

Column 1: Character Name
Column 2: Character Traits
Column 3: Page Number

You may find that some of your students visualize better when they draw a diagram of the set, or create charts with arrows, boxes, and circles. Periodically, invite them to share with their classmates the strategies they devise themselves to help them make sense of the text. Shared peer perceptions increase peer comprehension.

These notes and drawings can prepare students to participate actively in discussions about ways the playwrights unveil the personalities and motivations of characters. Writing and graphically representing these facts and impressions lead to deeper reading. They pay attention to the crucial information the dramatist reveals in the opening scenes, thus reducing confusion and frustration later.

Once these details are firm in their minds, students can read more confidently. Nevertheless, you probably have to remind them that reading a play is different from watching one. As readers, they must use all the clues the playwright gives in the dialogue and in the stage directions to imagine what the characters look like and what movements they may be making on stage.

GETTING THROUGH THE PLAY: ART, ACTING, AND VIDEO

Young people are more inclined to assume a persona when they have something to hold or feel they are disguised. Begin with a brief talk about which props or items of clothing would be appropriate for each character. If bringing props from home is unrealistic, ask to borrow some from the drama teacher and provide them yourself. You know to keep props simple and to avoid realistic-looking weapons—just much too tempting for shenanigans from mischievous adolescents.

Making Masks and Using Props

To get students to reflect more imaginatively on the personalities of the characters, have them make character masks using inexpensive paper plates and colored markers or crayons. Once you assemble the materials, they can complete the assignment in a single period, choosing colors and symbols that reflect the specific traits of their assigned characters. This creative artistic assignment reinforces learning and appeals to those who show what they know by drawing and those who learn by seeing.

This assignment also sends students back to the text. When they show their masks to the class, each student should quote the lines that substantiate their choice of color, symbol, or the pattern of images on their mask. These lines can be written neatly on the back of the mask, making them visible to mask makers as they describe their artistic depictions to the class.

Students often are surprised when peers choose the same color to symbolize different personality traits. With textual support, those choices are validated. In this case, cultural symbolism may have nothing to do with color choices, since most colors have both positive and negative connotations in any culture.

For example, with the play *Romeo and Juliet*, one student may choose red to reflect the love between Romeo and Rosalind, his lady love before Juliet. Another may use red to show the fiery temperament of Mercutio. A student may use black to represent Juliet's despair, while another uses black to represent the stubborn stance the Montagues and Capulets take on keeping their children apart.

The same holds true for symbols. When students support their choices with the text, most results make sense. One student may decorate her mask with birds to represent literally the swan and crow mentioned in the script and also to represent figuratively the flightiness of the characters. Another may use dog food bones to reflect Mercutio's speech about "a dog" and the "house of Montague." Neither the colors nor symbols students select are as important as the reasoning they offer based on the text. So much is revealed to them, their peers, and to you.

Whenever possible bring in appropriate, safe props and costume items for students to hold or wear while reading their parts aloud. For some reason, both props and costumes provide impetus for being more dramatic. The drama teacher may have some to loan. Students also may wish to bring in items to share. Using props and costume items reminds students that plays are written to be seen and heard.

Drawing, Playing with Childhood Toys, and Considering Music

Some teachers ask students to draw pictures or bring in pictures from magazines or newspapers to represent the play's characters. Others ask them what movie or television actors and actresses could be cast for certain parts. Of course, students should be asked to find evidence from the text of the play to support their choice of picture, actor, or actress. They may even design a playbill or suggest music for the dramatic work you have them read.

If this play were a musical, what style of music would be appropriate? Why? If it were a ballet, what would dances look like? These assignments call upon students' imagination and help them to connect and to contribute to the discussion inspired by their own creative ideas and their own artistic skills.

Further involve students and invite their input. Suggest that they bring in childhood toys and dolls to represent characters and scenes or spend a class period making sock puppets to use when reading a scene. What about using children's building blocks to re-create sets? Remember, your students may be teens who are still bridging the gap between childhood and adulthood. Playing with appropriate toys that they bring to class while studying a play may be just the thing to revive a play that may be dying on the vine. Even high school seniors get a kick out of being a kid once in a while.

Such activities reinforce learning by seeing, hearing and doing. Because students have written in the journals the words from the text and discussions, have experienced reading and hearing parts read, and have seen the visuals (photos or drawings in their text), they are more likely to remember the particulars of plot and theme and make connections between actions in plays and their own lives. These visual depictions also provide memory aids students may recall during written assessments and when they begin drafting their own plays.

DECIDING TO SHOW OR NOT TO SHOW

To supplement the study of a play, you may decide to show video clips. You could use clips of the same scenes from different productions—such as different versions of Hansberry's *A Raisin in the Sun*, or an English production and French version of *Cyrano de Bergerac*. In addition to using clips to give more insight into the setting, show a video clip of a conflict similar to one in the play you are reading. Afterward, ask the students to compare the way each set of characters responds to the conflict. Showing video of the play you are studying may be a good time for an in-context talk about the grammar of film. See Chapter Eight for reading the media.

COMPARING AND CONTRASTING FILM VERSIONS OF PLAYS

When you study *Cyrano de Bergerac*, for example, you could show video clips from both an English version of the play and the French version starring Gerard Depardieu. The French version can be advantageous even if students don't speak that language; they can pay attention to the action that is implied by the dialogue they've been reading.

The fact the French version is performed "in the field" and "on location" and not on stage provides an opportunity to discuss how stage and screen communicate differently—especially with lighting, close-ups, scene transitions, and audio/sound. This lesson may give students ideas about lighting and sound instructions to include when they flesh out scripts of their own plays.

Next ask students to discuss or write about the differences they note between the two media. Some are disappointed because they have imagined the people, places, and scenes to be different from what is shown in the video. This gives an opening to talk about the power of language to create images in our minds and the pleasure of reading widely and independently.

The key for you is to decide why the video clips are being shown and to determine whether they hurt or help students reach the standards for reading, viewing, and critical thinking laid out for the course. Sometimes more is just too much.

KEEPING THE PEACE
WHILE ENJOYING THE PLAY

As students get further into the play, they become eager to read aloud and act out the scenes. And because young people have a strong sense of fairness, it is important for you to be perceived as such. To be fair, arrange it so each one who wishes to read a "good" part has the opportunity to do so; keep a chart of who reads which part each day. At the end of each class period, during those closing ten minutes, you can write on the board or project a list of characters they are to meet in the next day's scene(s) and then ask for volunteers to prepare for the reading.

Those who have had small parts should have first choice for choosing the character they want to read the next day. Those who are scheduled to read ought to understand that they are expected to practice reading their lines aloud at home so they can read in character, without stumbling over unfamiliar words during class. Holding this casting session at the end of each class period is a subtle way of tantalizing them all to keep reading to find out what happens next and anticipating how well their classmates are going to interpret the upcoming scenes.

If practice at home is not realistic in your school setting, invite the readers to come before or after school and practice in your room. Teens abhor embarrassment, so they take seriously their responsibility of bringing alive the characters in front of their peers. Meetings like this can be a great opportunity for you to have one-on-one time or get to work with a smaller group of students.

The challenge will be to have established a classroom environment that supports even the stumbling reader and the English-Language Learner student whose articulation may not be as easy to understand as native speakers. Do what you can to give each volunteer an opportunity to read aloud in class. The students have their texts in front of them, so they can follow along as though viewing a film with closed captions.

Chapter 7

ACTING OUT SCENES
AND CREATING MORE TABLEAUX

Allotting time to act out the scenes is particularly important to ensure that your teaching appeals to multiple intelligences—especially your visual, auditory, and kinesthetic learners. To demonstrate the ways that dialogue demands certain action and activity, you could give the same scene to multiple groups and ask them to do a dramatic reading that includes some staging and movement. If your class tends to be noisy with talkative teens, how about assigning them to present scenes silently, with pantomime only! Then, after they present the scene, ask the group members to justify their choices for acting or reacting.

Creating tableaux again of the later scenes in the play further reinforces student understanding of the relationships of characters one to another. This time, raise the level of reflection and observation and ask students to pay attention to posture as well as position in relation to another character.

One may have a dominant character standing, a neutral one sitting, and a subservient one kneeling. They may decide to have one character standing farther away from the audience and another nearer, depending on the mood of the scene. In a quiet scene, ask the students to decide what gestures would be appropriate during a particular speech. What would the non-speaking characters be doing during that speech? Why?

Drop in on groups as they plan scenes to act out

You can maintain more consistent control in the classroom during acting scenes by planning backward—clarify for yourself what you expect to accomplish when you schedule lessons for the students to act out scenes. (1) Consider the dynamics of each class: how have they interacted in prior situations? (2) Give clear directions before "letting them loose," and (3) circulate among them as they work. (4) Set your timer to signal about five minutes before the end of the period—that way, you can call the students back to order and conduct a short oral reflection on what they learned by acting out the scene.

When they know what is expected, what is allowed or not allowed, and know that you are nearby to help them behave themselves, they usually live up to your expectations. You can achieve your goals and retain your sense of humor.

DEEPENING UNDERSTANDING OF LITERARY DEVICES

By the second semester, your students are at ease identifying, discussing, and writing about most literary devices except theme and irony. So when you plan lessons for drama study, design activities to help them develop greater confidence with these features of literature. You could quiz them with quotations from the play and ask students to identify the speaker, situation, and importance of that speech to characterization, plot advancement, or setting. These informal assessments measure their retention of this knowledge.

To understand and identify literary themes in plays, students must understand the plot line. They may find it useful first to refer to their one-paragraph summaries of the five Ws and H questions. Just as you taught during the short story unit, ask them to write thematic statements in which they identify the universal situation based on the conflict, and the universal response to the situation based on the character's response to the conflict.

It may help them write these theme statements by reminding them of what they learned in the short story unit. For those who need it, provide a sample formatted sentence with missing words:

When people_____ (students fill in the situation), they _____ (students fill in the response to the situation).

For one homework assignment, ask your students to try writing some of these sentences in their reading journals or digital notebooks. After they write the theme statements, they can later convert the SWBST phrases (*Somebody Wanted, But, So, Then*) into simple sentences that generalize the concept captured in their preliminary drafts. Students soon recognize the universal quality of plays in much the way they saw them in other literary works studied this school year.

Statements about theme in *Cyrano de Bergerac* from a seventh grader's journal:

- When people have a crush on someone, they show off for their crush. (In some neighborhoods "crush" is also slang for the object of one's affections.)
- When someone dies, their loved ones mourn for them.
- People respond to tense situations with brave action.
- People are willing to battle physically or emotionally to get what they want.
- People with physical flaws try to impress others to avoid rejection.
- People are attracted first to external features.

WRITING PLAYS AND CROSS-CURRICULAR COLLABORATIONS

Students learn well when they see a link to other topics or subjects they are studying in other classes. Collaborating teachers who take time to create such lessons tend to have more success in getting their students to engage. One activity that lends itself well to cross-curricular collaboration is playwriting.

For example, in many schools eighth graders study physical science that includes units on geology, weather, and the planets. Many eighth-grade literature lists include legends and myths. What a wonderful opportunity to write plays based on those myths that attempt to explain early man's rationale for the way the earth is formed, what causes weather, how stars came to be arranged in distinctive patterns, and why the planets exist.

The same kind of teaming could work with colleagues in the history or social studies department. Students could write plays about historical people and events. Invite a teacher in the other department to work with you to design a joint assignment for which your students write a play set in the same historical period or features the real people they may be studying in one of those other classes, like art, music, and physical education. Then you can share the grading using the features of the familiar Six Traits rubric or one that teachers from both departments create together.

For example, one of you could read the student-written plays for accuracy of facts and ideas, for voice and sentence fluency. The other could read for organization, word choice, and conventions of drama writing as well as for mechanics, usage, and grammar. Such sharing could halve the labor and double the pleasure of working together on a project that enhances authenticity of assessment in both areas of study.

After studying a group of short stories, you may be ready to introduce students to playwriting instead of short story writing. Small groups could choose different short stories already studied and then create a script based on one of the short stories and incorporate the elements of drama they learn in this drama unit. Students may find it helpful to use such questions as those that follow to self-check their progress in playwriting on the topic you assign or they choose.[4]

BOX 7.1 PLAYWRITING CHECK-UP LIST

These also are questions students could consider about peer drafts during read-around groups or in-class peer feedback created from this list.

- Is the plot focused on a single problem to be solved within a brief period of time?
- Is the personality of characters revealed primarily in dialogue; secondarily in action? (In other words, would a blind person be able to follow the flow of the story?)
- Does the dialogue introduce conflict early in the play?
- Does the dialogue sound like real conversation—brief, overlapping speeches and some fragments? (Here is a place for using local jargon, slang, and idioms.)
- Does the play have an identifiable beginning, middle, and end?
- Does the rising action include three increasingly more challenging obsta- cles in solving the problem?
- Is the climax realistic but not given away too soon?
- Does the resolution make sense based on the personality of characters?

Questions adapted from notes taken in Playwrights Project Workshop

---

If you begin planning early enough in the first semester, your drama teacher may have time to join forces with you and plan time for the drama classes in the second semester to perform selected dramas of your teen playwrights. You can imagine how gratifying it would be for these budding authors to see their words come to life! Knowing their work is to be seen by their peers, families, and/or friends encourages the students to do a better job on the assignment. Win. Win. Win.

SUMMATIVE ASSESSMENTS

At the end of the unit studying this genre of literature, you know to assess student learning by having students demonstrate their understanding of relationships among the characters, or the author's use of literary devices and the newly taught elements of drama. You could include options from which they can choose to

- summarize their learning by writing a poem about the play;
- write an additional scene describing what happens next with characters who have survived;
- write a one-act play with the same conflict set in a contemporary time or place;
- write a dramatic scene that reflects cultural celebration;
- take a test;
- write a paper;
- produce a video with live performers; or
- create an animated video to post on your class website.

CONCLUSION

The study of drama can be an enriching experience for students and teachers because it incorporates six language arts skills: reading, writing, speaking, listening, representing, viewing and using technology—and provides a reason to practice cooperative learning. Moreover, while reading drama students get to see how literary concepts earlier learned are used in another genre of literature. Finally, drama is just fun because it reflects so many cultures and appeals to a wide range of students across the range of multiple intelligences and especially those who like to talk, to watch, to move, and to act up. Who's left?

Yes—by the time you have completed a series of lessons with drama, you may find yourself quoting Cyrano's line, "I order you to be silent!" With your careful planning, your students become so excited about playing their parts that you may need to "write down their names" and they each will want to be "at the top of the list." When you issue the challenge to "Step forward, young heroes!" even the shyer students volunteer to be a part of the fun and be ready to "break a leg."

NOTES

1. Edmond Rostand, *Cyrano de Bergerac,* trans. Lowell Blair, *World Literature* (Lake Forest: Glencoe: Macmillan/McGraw-Hill, 1991), 472.

2. *Cyrano de Bergerac* (with English subtitles). Starring: Gérard Depardieu, Anne Brochet, Director: Jean-Paul Rappeneau. Format: Color, NTSC Rated: PG. Studio: Mgm/Ua Studios, Video Release Date: February 21, 2000.

3. *Core Standards,* 2011. http://www.corestandards.org/assets/CCSSI_ELA%20 Standards.pdf (accessed September 16, 2018).

4. See companion website for ideas to a playwriting unit, http://teachingenglish languagearts.com/.

Chapter 8

Unreeling Nonfiction: Essays, Speeches, and the Media

When we begin to realize that there is just as much creativity that goes into writing nonfiction as there is in fiction, we can truly appreciate it.[1]

—from "The Importance of Non-Fiction," by Rachel Peterson

If you are like some English language arts teachers educated in the mid-twentieth century, you may not have considered nonfiction when you began thinking about teaching genres. Back then, genres more often referred to fictional literature, and literature is what one taught in English classes. Strange, though, that most students were asked to write essays.

However, as that century wound down and the twenty-first century began, more and more educators recognized the value of teaching students to read essays as a genre, write and present their thinking as public speeches, and share what they were learning in mediums using various electronic devices. This change in perspective made understanding how media work a critical component of language arts instruction.

This chapter is designed to demonstrate ways to build into your course lessons that have students learning the language of nonfiction, analyzing essays, media, and speeches, thus understanding better the unique traits of yet another broad genre—nonfiction—and three of its subcategories. You need not be left reeling when you prepare to teach these literary types.

THE ESSAY

Essays are a short literary composition that reflects the author's outlook or point. A short literary composition on a particular theme or subject, usually in prose and generally analytic, speculative, or interpretative.[2]

Understanding *how* to read nonfiction is key

The term "essay" comes from the French word meaning "to try." Originally, this descriptor for nonfiction referred to writers' attempts to articulate their thoughts on specific topics. As the printing press made writing more widely accessible to the public, more and more people began writing and publishing their thinking about politics, religion, and science. Many more schools found that textbooks could be printed and distributed for student use as a supplement to the lecturing that had occurred in prominent colleges and universities.

Over time, recurring traits began to appear in this writing, and the public began to expect essays to reflect specific structural features and patterns of organization. Just as genres of fiction have distinctive qualities that differentiate them from one another, nonfiction essays, speeches, and the media have their own set of literary terminology that identifies these characteristics. You may know these as text structures, traits of public speaking, and the grammar of media, which usually refers to messaging that uses visual images, movement, and color. These components are manipulated in different ways to achieve specific purposes communicating with identifiable audiences.

PERITEXT IN TEXTBOOKS

Your students may recognize some text features in expository nonfiction works and may need to be reminded of ways these features work in their text books and on websites. In that first case, they are paying attention to chapter titles, images that may be added to certain pages, diagrams, maps, charts, or unexpected spacing that sometimes appears in fiction. Chapter titles often signal what is to come.

Your students may also have noticed that authors of modern fiction sometimes choose to write from multiple points of view, and the only clue to these changes may be an extra space between paragraphs or a flourish or line to indicate this shift in perspective. Readers may be confused if they miss these subtle peritext cues. These signals sometimes are used in nonfiction, too.

Learning to Use Text Structure

If text structures are not defined or explained in your anthology, check out websites that include definitions and mini-lessons to help you get started. Most suggest that teachers

- introduce the idea that expository texts have a text structure;
- introduce common text structures of (1) sequence/chronological order, (2) classification, (3) definition, (4) process, (5) description, (6) comparison, (7) problem/solution, and (8) cause/effect;
- show examples of paragraphs that correspond to each text structure;
- examine topic sentences and signal words that clue the reader to a specific structure;
- model the writing of a paragraph that uses a specific structure; and
- have students try writing paragraphs that follow a structure.

For students who are proficient with paragraph organization, do the last three steps in the preceding list with longer chunks of text or entire chapters, as suggested by the National Education Association.

Students often miss signal words that help process the ideas presented in essays; reviewing those is helpful, too. The Internet is an excellent resource for fleshing out your lists of signal words based on the age, skills, and needs of your students. There you will find appropriate charts that include such words and phrases as, for example, *first, then, furthermore, on the other hand, consequently, finally*, and so on.

Remember the chapter on poetry, where you read that poetry is someone saying something to someone? That's the case with essays, too. As you teach your students to read and understand essays, have them try to discover the following:

- Who is speaking?
- For what general purpose: to inform, argue, persuade, entertain, or commemorate?

Misunderstanding values leads to misunderstanding peers

- With what message?
- To what audience?
- How does the writer organize the essay to achieve that purpose?
- What rhetorical devices has the author employed for that audience?

UNDERSTANDING THE ROLE OF VALUES

An exercise that helps students consider purpose and audience relates to values. By carefully inspecting word choice, sentence syntax, and organization, readers can discover what is important to the essay writer. They can get a hint at what the audience thinks is important, too. Your question to students is, "how do you, the reader, know?" For the most part, any answer students can validate and support with evidence from the text and logical reasons should be accepted. This is where P.I.E. structures help reduce arguments among those who may disagree.

You recall with this approach to speaking and writing, the students state their POSITION or opinion, next ILLUSTRATE with EXAMPLES from the beginning, middle, and end of the text, and then, EXPLAIN ways those references support their position/opinion. Explaining is the most important element because it shows their level of understanding.

A LESSON ON VALUES

Prepare your students to read more deeply, gaining more insight from fewer readings. Step back a moment before you have them analyzing articles, reading and listening to speeches, viewing video and media about controversial issues. Develop a short presentation on values. This is an opportunity for the class to look at what people value and think is important for us and those we care about; what influences our behavior and colors our lenses when we read, listen, and view communication in any form.

Here is a one-period lesson during which you and your class create a word cloud:

- Distribute a list of forty to fifty value words you compile from sources on the Internet.
- Ask students to circle ten words that represent their own values.
- Redistribute these anonymous lists to students on opposite sides of the room (left side gets right side's lists, and vice versa).
- Have them read that list aloud, while one student volunteer—an accurate and speedy word-processor—enters all the words as they are read. Repetition is fine. The number of times a word appears on the final list will determine the size the word will appear in the word cloud created in Wordle, or whatever online cloud creator you choose.
- Copy and paste the class list of value words into an online web program like wordle.net. This application will create a word cloud that shows the primary values of your class.
- Project the word cloud in silence. Allow students to view it for a full sixty seconds before verbalizing and discussing their class cloud of values.

It will be enlightening for your students to see the range of values among their peers. After hearing and seeing what the class believes is important, they will have a common language to write and talk about these controversial topics. Often when students see these kinds of differences, they can understand why intelligent, thoughtful people disagree on topics important to them both. Your students may find it interesting to read pro/con essays found on this website: http://www.procon.org/.

Then, using that same list of value words, ask students to consider what writers of the articles and speeches and creators of media value. Ask students to point out words, phrases, images, note what's missing, and who's quoted, and so on. Equally informative for readers is thinking about what the target audience values and ways the writer/creator recognizes and/or appeals to those values.

This lesson on discovering values works well with 1 described in chapter 1 on "Responding to Literature"—"Nine Yardsticks"—that structured way to look at, evaluate, and critique literature. One of the yardsticks is PERSONAL BELIEFS, which considers the fact that personal beliefs determine how people respond to what they read, hear, and view.

READING PERSUASIVE ESSAYS AND SPEECHES

Providing students with probing questions helps them read essays and speeches, and eventually apply similar strategies when writing their own ideas to publish or present in person or online. For example, if you assign them to read an essay or speech to persuade, remind them that most persuasive writing includes information for the audience to learn, arguments to make them contemplate, and calls for actions to persuade them to change their thinking or behavior. Then, have pairs of students read the sample text to determine the kinds of arguments they notice by way of the *head*, *heart*, and/or *pocket*:

- Does this writer make appeals to the *head* (definitions, statistics, explanations, and comparison/contrast)?
- Does this writer make appeals to the *heart* (humor, explanations, illustrations, quotations, testimony, or stories about real people)?
- Does this writer make appeals to the *pocket* (definitions, facts, statistics, and comparison/contrast related to money)?

You may recall these in a more formal light as Aristotle's rhetorical devices of ethos, logos, and pathos. If your students are ready, go ahead and introduce this vocabulary to discuss argumentation and persuasion. When they write, insist that they use ethical arguments that do not devolve into use of fallacies they see in some commercials and political rantings such as

- ad hominem fallacy,
- straw man,
- appeal to ignorance,
- false dilemma/false dichotomy,
- slippery slope,
- circular argument,
- hasty generalization,
- red herring, and/or
- bandwagoning.

Compelling Arguments

Appeal to head...

...heart...

...and pocket.

Persuasive essays may have arguments that appeal to head, heart, and pocket

MEDIA GRAMMAR

For decades English language arts educators have taught students the grammar rules for writing and the grammar rules of literature (plot structure for fiction and text structure for nonfiction) but only recently have they begun to teach the grammar of media. Twenty-first-century students view other print and electronic media many more hours per day than they view/read traditional books.

For this reason, you are beginning to see media literacy among the standards to which you are to teach and in the Common Core Standards for English language arts. The anchor standards require curricula to include assessment that determines how well students can "integrate and evaluate information presented in diverse media and formats, including visually, quantitatively, and orally."[3] You can design lessons to teach your students how to "read the media" found in magazines and films, as well as on websites.

Knowing media grammar leads to critical viewing

Lots of resources are on the Internet on such sites as Edutopia.org that include interviews about the value of teaching the grammar of media literacy and a variety of video clips to use for classroom instruction. You can just use magazines you collect and keep in your classroom, or digital files of images you compile and project in electronic slide programs like PowerPoint or Prezi.

Some simple lessons introduce students to the use of color and layout. Other more in-depth lessons may involve learning the language of film—camera angles, use of lighting, timing of shots, and numbers of cuts—viewing samples as a class, and then in groups, and assign students to create short video or web pages that illustrate the concepts you are teaching.

Deconstructing the Grammar of Media

Deconstruction, a collection of lesson plans developed by the Center for Media Literacy (CML), includes five key questions and five core concepts.[4]

Five key questions:

1. Who created this message?
2. What creative techniques are used to attract my attention?

3. How might different people understand this message differently?
4. What values, lifestyles, and points of view are represented in, or omitted from, this message?
5. Why is this message being sent?

Five core concepts:

1. All media messages are constructed.
2. Media messages are constructed using a creative language with its own rules.
3. Different people experience the same media message differently.
4. Media have embedded values and points of view.
5. Most media messages are organized to gain profit and/or power.

Becoming critical viewers is just the first step in understanding and learning how to read the media. Producing that media is the step that shows that learning is taking place.

Assessing News Grammar

This news-related assignment requires students to conduct research, practice citation and documentation, and think more critically about persuasive techniques. During the first two weeks of this month-long assignment that can be combined with a fiction unit, readers are to select a topic reported in a print or digital medium, then bring in copies of four or five written articles. They can also use text transcriptions of television reports available on local and network websites.

If your students have access to the Internet, they can follow the news easily. The purpose is to have them follow the news for a month and be prepared to assess ways the nonfiction writing is the same and/or different from the text structure of fiction being studied in class.

After they have read opening chapters of the fiction work the class is studying, are through the exposition of that text, and have a solid sense of the personalities of the characters, you could ask students to write a brief rationale to explain why a particular literary character would be interested in some current event and what would be that character's response to those particular news stories. For example:

- Why would Jem in *To Kill a Mockingbird* be interested in a trial reported in news media? What would he say about the verdict?

- Why would Mercutio or Benvolio in *Romeo and Juliet* be interested in curfew laws that require teenagers to be at home before 10 p.m.? What arguments for and against them?
- Why would Panchito from *The Circuit* or Esperanza from *Esperanza Rising* be interested in educational opportunities for undocumented immigrants? How would they advocate for more?

As you and the class continue studying the novel, students can be gathering information to flesh out persuasive speeches, or they could read and reflect on a speech in your class based on a topic they are studying in history, science, music, or math. Consider having them pattern the structure of a speech they like and present it as an example of a speech to inform, persuade, entertain, or commemorate. The introduction to their presentation should identify the rhetorical devices they are using and the text structures they will demonstrate.

Depending on your school setting and the access your students have to resources, you may need to allot in-class time for research as well as for practicing the speeches once they are written.

This kind of multigenre and interdisciplinary assignment—looking at fiction and nonfiction concurrently in both print and electronic media—helps students make text-world connections to see that times change but people don't: a universal quality of good literature. Since a portion of the assignment requires them to justify their reasons for choosing the kinds of news articles and relating them to fictional characters, this assignment requires your student readers to consider the ways their fiction authors reveal the personalities and motivations of characters in the novels.

Finally, incorporating a speech based on real news articles in the same instructional unit as the study of a novel gives students a chance to detect the different text structures used in fiction and nonfiction, a critical-thinking skill most schools expect maturing students to acquire.

GIVING AN ORAL REPORT OR PRESENTING A SPEECH?

Are you one of the English teachers who bemoan the fact that you find it a challenge to teach students to give a "good" speech? Like other colleagues in your department, do you acknowledge that students do well on "oral reports," yet something still is lacking? Speech-giving really is different from giving an oral report. But how?

Ask your students a few questions and the features become clear. Start your unit on reading and presenting public speeches asking your savvy students what they notice about a good speaker. Surprisingly, they seldom comment on the content of the speech, but instead point out aspects of delivery like giving verbal clues to organization pattern, making eye contact, using gestures, rate of speaking, clear articulation, varied intonation, poise, and so on.

Of course, middle school students probably do not use these terms, but what they mention clearly shows that *how* the report is delivered is the key feature that makes the speech an effective one. Therefore, if you expect them to become effective, competent, and confident speakers, it seems only right that you incorporate into your lesson planning opportunities for students to observe and critique good speaking and also the time to write and practice their own speeches.

Ask your students to watch television news reporters. Find and show them short video clips of politicians, and businessmen and businesswomen delivering speeches. Watch an inspirational speaker giving a talk. Websites such as TED Talks include presentations on a range of topics by an even wider range of speakers. With careful screening, you will find videos appropriate and inspiring for use in your school classroom regardless of how homogenous or diverse the student population may be.

Urge your students to watch their teachers. Encourage them to pay attention to the delivery styles of their imams, pastors, priests, and rabbis. After just a few observations, your student monitors can assemble a list of those characteristics of content, structure, style and vocal qualities that make oral presentations simple to follow and easy to remember. Next, encourage them to pattern effective deliveries that fit their own personal style.

Preparing and presenting speeches demonstrates understanding

Presenting a Speech

Giving a speech is more than reading an essay aloud. An effective speech is both an oral and visual presentation designed for a specific audience, place, and purpose. Since public speaking is designed to be heard, few listeners come prepared to take notes. They will retain more of what they hear if the content and delivery are designed to help listeners know what to listen for, and also provide spoken cues to remind listeners of what they have heard. Effective speakers dress for the occasion and use voice and physical qualities to enhance what is being said.

During your study of the text of speeches, students probably recognize the speech writers include more repetition to guide audience in following, comprehending, and recalling ideas presented. They notice use of shorter, more declarative sentences comprised of vivid verbs, concrete nouns, and graphic images. Speech writers carefully choose vocabulary chosen for its sound and suggestive power. Sound familiar? Remember the definition of poetry in Chapter Six?

By this time, your students will also point out that carefully chosen transitions help hold the speech together while keeping the listeners on track with the positions, arguments, and stories being presented in informative, persuasive, and entertaining speeches. These transitions often are the same signal words students learned in their study of text structure in essays. See, they are noticing the similarities in the various genres of literature, even those they are being taught as distinctive kinds of writing.

A thoughtful speaker takes into consideration what the audience sees as it listens. This begins with attire, gestures, and use of physical space. The speakers also practice their speeches often enough to be able to deliver it in a pace that is easy to follow, using pauses, pacing, and volume to attract and retain attention throughout the speech.

Consider showing video of short speeches to demonstrate these distinguishing traits of a public speech versus the oral reading of an essay. After the first minute, turn off the volume and let students just watch the speaker for a couple of minutes before raising the volume again. They will get the picture.

Speaking for Different Purposes

Generally, there are four basic kinds of speeches—to inform, to persuade, to entertain, and to commemorate—and during the course of a school year you can ask students to read, then prepare, and present one of each. You do not have to wait until later in the school year to have a formal speech unit of two or three weeks, assignments for analysis of speeches, and the time to complete their presentations. While elements of preparation and practice both are keys to effective public presentations, having given oral presentations throughout the year students have personal experience to reflect upon when you begin direct instruction about public speaking.

Picking a Topic and Planning a Speech

For older students, you may design a news-related speech assignment where they are expected to think critically about authentic purposes for persuasive speaking, conduct research, use correct citation and documentation, then write and present a speech on a current issue. In this case, too, you can link the assignment to a piece of literature you are studying.

For example, you may have assigned the lesson for which students select a news-related topic that might interest one of the characters from a novel or article the class has read or is studying. Later in the year, you may have them write and present a speech to address a problem in the school or community. They generally respond enthusiastically, willing to practice their newly developed skills when allowed to apply them on a social justice topic relevant or important to them. Offer them the option of giving the speech in the persona of a fictional character. Doing so gives students a safe mask and distance between a controversial topic and their class as audience.

Getting Off to a Good Start and Using a Variety of Evidence

As students read published speeches and then pattern them for speeches of their own, have them use questions like those that follow to discover what makes the persuasive speech they read effective:

1. Does this speech open with an attention getter than makes the audience want to listen?
2. Does the introduction include *sign posts* or *signal words* that indicate the order of the arguments to follow?
3. Does this speech clearly show that this topic is important to me (personally or as the character)?

4. Does this speech clearly show why this topic is important to the members of my real or fictional audience?
5. Does this speech provide adequate support for each main section of the speech? (Check the number of times the speech writer includes each of these supporting materials in the speech.)

_____ illustrations/examples	_____ explanations
_____ definitions	_____ restatements
_____ statistics/numbers	_____ humor
_____ comparison/contrast	_____ opinion of experts
_____ testimony	_____ quotations

Having students make a script of their speech is a practical way to have them practice the grammar of Standard English they have been learning, too. Their goal is to communicate clearly both in writing and in speaking in an appropriate grammar, Standard English, or otherwise. Their choice of grammar makes the difference in how well they get their ideas across to their audience even if their purpose is to entertain peers in their class commemorating a character in a story, a historical figure in history, a real

Presenting speech in person of character can reduce nervousness

friend, or family member. If they choose not to use Standard English, ask them to articulate why the language they choose is appropriate for their purpose and audience.

Practicing, Practicing, Practicing

Insist that your students get feedback on their speeches before presenting them in class for evaluation. This listener could be a friend or family member, or if that is not reasonable to expect in the setting where you teach, this someone could be a classmate. Practicing aloud is the only way for them to know for certain they are familiar enough with content of their speech to deliver it with confidence, making eye contact, using gestures, pronouncing words correctly and clearly, varying the pace of the speaking, and maintaining their poise.

Students sometimes wonder what they should be paying attention to when they practice a speech, so plan on providing a few guidelines to assure these soon-to-be orators that they are on the right track. Strongly suggest that they time themselves as they give their speech at least three times standing in front of a mirror, holding their notes on the same index cards they plan to use when they give their speech in public. If they can look up at themselves and keep talking through their speech, they probably are prepared to look up and make more frequent eye contact with their audience.

Share with student speakers that the criteria on which their oral presentations will be assessed, includeing traits like CONTENT, ORGANIZATION, VOCAL FEATURES, and APPEARANCE. See figure 8.1 for organizing a week of speeches with color groups of four or five students who write peer feedback on one trait each day, except the day their color group is presenting. This structure also works well for other kinds of in-class presentations of projects.

Encourage your students to wear something special on the day they give the speech, an outfit that is especially neat, comfortable, and appropriate for their intended audience. Choosing what to wear reminds them that people in an audience are spectators, also influenced by the speaker's physical appearance and posture. When resources are available at home or at school, recommend that your students make an audio or video recording and listen and watch to hear and see what others will hear and see when they deliver their speeches.

Students who are asked to give a little more attention to observing; assigned to point out the qualities of a good speech; and given time to research, write, and practice become attuned to differences in effectiveness. These young communicators no longer are content simply to give a report, but endeavor to present a speech.

Day	Red	Green	Purple	Orange	Blue
1	SPEAKING No feedback	CONTENT Feedback on (e.g.): • appropriateness for audience • variety of support • appeals • quality of evidence and resources sources cited	ORGANIZATION Feedback on (e.g.): • introduction SIGN POST (statement of purpose) • TRANSITIONS • appropriateness for kind of speech • CONCLUSION (summary, reflection, or projection without introducing new ideas)	VOCAL ISSUES Feedback on (e.g.): • articulation • intonation • pace • pauses • volume	APPEARANCE Feedback on (e.g.): • appropriate gestures • use of physical space • visual aids
2	APPEARANCE	SPEAKING	CONTENT	ORGANIZATION	VOCAL ISSUES
3	VOCAL ISSUES	APPEARANCE	SPEAKING	CONTENT	ORGANIZATION
4	ORGANIZATION	VOCAL ISSUES	APPEARANCE	SPEAKING	CONTENT
5	CONTENT	ORGANIZATION	VOCAL ISSUES	APPEARANCE	SPEAKING

Figure 8.1 Organize week of speeches with color groups

CONCLUSION

Teaching students to read essays, listen to speeches, and view media with a critical eye helps them become defensive readers, listeners, viewers, and thoughtful creators in a variety of formats. They become more sensitive to the impact color, size, and design have on those with whom they wish to communicate when given the opportunity to create and present to their classmates on topics that matter to them.

Students will also be able to travel with ease across this country and abroad, fairly certain they can handle the demands of reading, hearing, and viewing complex texts because they understand these nonfiction genres, and can even create them with relative confidence and competence. As they mature and enter the world of work, your students are not likely to be passed up for a job promotion simply because they lack the reading, speaking, and media skills called for in most school standards for English language arts and sought in the twenty-first-century job markets. But most important, your students will be prepared to speak up and speak out on issues that matter to them today, with the assurance that you are teaching them to be sensitive and successful in any setting.

NOTES

1. Rachel Peterson, "The Importance of Non-Fiction," *Odyssey*, March 29, 2016. https://www.theodysseyonline.com/importance-nonfiction (accessed September 15, 2018).
2. "Genres of Literature." http://genresofliterature.com/ (accessed July 5, 2018).
3. *Common Core State Standards Initiative*. http://www.corestandards.org/ELA-Literacy/CCRA/SL/2/ (accessed September 15, 2018).
4. Fred Baker, "CML's Five Key Questions and Core Concepts of Media Literacy for Deconstruction." Media Lit, 2011. http://www.medialit.org/reading-room/five-key-questions-form-foundation-media-inquiry (accessed September 16, 2018).

Afterword

Safe Travels: Acknowledge the Challenge and Maximize the Opportunity

> Ideal teachers are those who use themselves as bridges over which they invite their students to cross, then having facilitated their crossing, joyfully collapse, encouraging them to create bridges of their own.[1]
>
> —Nikos Kazantzakis

Whether you are beginning your first, second, seventh, or seventeenth year of teaching, you are set to embark on a trip of a lifetime. Each year of teaching can be different, unique, and surprisingly very much the same—an opportunity to learn and to inspire learning.

Language arts, you know, is the one course students take nearly every year they are in school. Those who teach them well come to appreciate the time and flexibility to adjust instruction in ways that enhance student learning across the curriculum and thus increase student enjoyment of schooling in general. Really?

The core components of the language arts curriculum—reading, writing, speaking, and listening—are skills that form the foundation for learning in all other academic courses. Proficiency in these areas is expected when youngsters enter their middle school social studies, science, and math classes. By the time they reach higher grades, students are expected to recognize distinctions between various genres and specific literary terms, enabling them to talk about both fiction and nonfiction and write with self-assurance in any course they take.

When such aptitude is missing or deficient, language arts teachers usually are called on the carpet to explain why they are not doing their job. How should you respond? What can you do to reduce the angst when accused of being an ineffective educator?

First, acknowledge the challenge of teaching genres to a diverse student body. Yes—you may have middle school students in the throes of puberty, dealing with raging hormones, startling physical changes or lack thereof; distressing emotional roller coasters; and uncertainty about figuring out what all these different teachers want from them! Or you may have adults returning to school after years away from academic work, uncomfortable with the unknown, wondering if they can cut it.

For the first time, some middle school students have multiple teachers daily. There is not just one teacher who knows what Sui Ming likes and dislikes and how she learns best; a teacher who makes allowances for Harold when he's just moved from living with dad for six months into the house with mom, her current husband and new baby; or one teacher who understands Juanita freezes when asked to read out loud without having time to practice. These students may have to learn their way around a larger school and even find a place to eat lunch with people they don't even know. How can they attend to class work?

You may have adult students who are pulled by myriad outside distractions on their jobs, in their homes, and from their families. Still, Leilani and Ahmed endeavor to learn enough to advance themselves and prepare for demanding new careers.

At the same time, language arts teachers have a curriculum to complete, a set of course standards to see that each student reaches, and parents and administrators who expect them to show in their grading the growth of each student. How can teachers of diverse student bodies be professionally effective and personally satisfied enough to feel successful as classroom teachers?

Maximize the opportunity. Students want to learn, and they thrive with educators willing to learn how to teach them—as individuals, not as receptacles of information. Research in the past twenty years has revealed what experienced teachers have suspected: their classes reflect multiple intelligences and students who learn in different ways; culture makes a difference; males learn better in certain settings than females do. The researchers urge teachers to adapt instruction to enhance all learning. No—this does not mean creating individualized educational plans for every student you teach. It does mean designing lessons that teach the same lesson in a variety of ways and offers students choices in how they show what they know.

You are not alone on this journey even within your classroom. Your students are there to help. They may know the school, the community, and neighborhood better than you, so let them teach you the ropes, but keep in mind that you are a professional. You are the educator hired to see that you all have safe passage along the sometimes-rocky road that is a year in the life of your travel mates.

Keep your eyes on the goal and, using your peripheral vision, keep your students in view, too. They are who you are teaching. Yes—you are teaching people, not just content. With patience and persistence, you all can reach the journey's end safely, secure in the knowledge you have gained and the skills you have honed.

How can you be assured that you can reach the destination intact?

- By carefully planning lessons based on what you know about the curriculum and what you learn about your students each school year.
- By observing and documenting what goes on in your classes.
- By varying the kind of performance and product assessments you assign.
- By being willing to modify your lessons to meet the needs and interests of your students.
- By being firm but fair in your interactions with students, colleagues, parents, and guardians.
- By recognizing that help is available—right in this book, and right in your classroom and from your students, your fellow travelers on this journey.
- By taking time each week to refresh yourself, spending time with family and friends or reading a book you don't have to teach.
- By attending—every year—at least one conference, seminar, or workshop for professional and personal enrichment.
- By believing that associating with excited, enthusiastic, and experienced educators is the best way to maintain your passion for the profession.

Know that as you teach your students to understand and use the language arts to receive knowledge and to express themselves, you are giving them the golden tickets to academic success and personal satisfaction. You, their language arts teacher, have the privilege of guiding and coaching each one along the journey. You, who provide the balance between dependable discipline and appropriate play in a safe, supportive environment, can help raise their self-esteem and increase their confidence and competence in communicating in culturally relevant ways.

Whether you are teaching English language arts here because it is your dream job or until you get an assignment teaching in another educational setting, or choose a different career path—do what you can to make these crucial years for students ones during which they learn to love learning because you have recognized the challenge and are maximizing the opportunity to enjoy and teach each student as a unique individual.

Each time you design flexible lessons permeated with (1) rich experiences for exploring fiction and nonfiction in the print and electronic media; (2) writing in a range of modes for a variety of authentic purposes; (3) talking and listening to you, their peers, and those they encounter face-to-face and online;

Careful planning leads to less-stressful travel

and (4) learning to critically view and use technology, you are cultivating in them vital skills for growth. With diligence on your part and assiduousness on theirs, you all will complete a school year inspired by the success of the current year, eager to move on to the challenges of the next. So, safe travels! Enjoy the journey!

NOTE

1. Nikos Kazantzakis, "Quotes by Nikos Kazantzakis." *Good Reads,* 2011. http://www.goodreads.com/quotes/show/301968 (accessed April 5, 2012).

Bibliography

Academy of American Poets. http://www.poets.org/index.php (December 18, 2018).
Advanced Dictionary. Sunnyvale, CA: Thorndike-Barnhart Series, 1988.
Asian Pacific Economic Cooperation. "21st Century Competencies." http://hrd.apec wiki.org/index.php/21st_Century_Competencies (March 16, 2012).
Assembly on Literature for Adolescents. "ALAN Online: The Official Site of the Assembly on Literature for Adolescents." http://www.ncte.org/adlit (March 16, 2012).
Baines, Lawrence. "Cool Books for Tough Guys: 50 Books Out of the Mainstream of Adolescent Literature That Will Appeal to Males Who Do Not Enjoy Reading." *The Alan Review* 22, no. 1 (1994).
Baker, F. "Media Awareness Network. 2010." http://www.media-awareness.ca/eng lish/teachers/media_literacy/key_concept.cfm (March 27, 2012).
Baker, F. "Media Literacy: One of the 21st Century Skills Your Students Need." *Palmetto Administrator Magazine* (2005).
Ballator, Nada, Marisa Farnum, and Bruce Kaplan. "NAEP 1996 Trends in Writing: Fluency and Writing Conventions." *NAEP 1996 Trends in Writing: Fluency and Writing Conventions* (1998).
Beers, Kylene. "The Measure of Our Success." In *Adolescent Literacy: Turning Promise into Practice*, 2007.
Beers, Kylene, Robert E. Probst, and Linda Reif. *Adolescent Literacy: Turning Promise into Practice*. Portsmouth, NH: Heinemann, 2007.
Blau, Sheridan. *The Literature Workshop: Teaching Texts and Their Readers*. Portsmouth, NH: Heinemann, 2003.
Blum, Joshua, Bob Holman, and Mark Pellington. *The United States of Poetry*. New York: Henry N. Holt, 1996.
Borron, B. "My Name, My Self: Using Name to Explore Identity." In *Reading, Thinking, and Writing about Multicultural Literature*, Carol B. Olson. Glenview, IL: Scott Foresman, 1996.

Bransford, John D., Ann L. Brown, and Rodney R. Cockin. *How People Learn: Brain, Mind, Experience, and School.* Washington, DC: National Academy Press, 2000.

Burke, Edmund. "Quotes and Sayings about Books and Reading." The Quote Garden. http://www.quotegarden.com/books.html (September 7, 2009).

Burke, Jim. *The English Teacher's Companion: A Complete Guide to Classroom, Curriculum, and the Profession.* Portsmouth, NH: Heinemann, 2007.

Burke, Jim. "Teaching English Language Arts in a Flat World." In *Adolescent Literacy: Turning Promise into Practice*, K Beers R. Probst, and L. Reif. Portsmouth, NH: Heinemann, 2007.

Busching, Beverly, and Betty Ann Slesinger. *"It's Our World Too": Socially Responsive Learners in Middle School Language Arts.* Urbana, IL: National Council of Teachers of English, 2002.

Carrasquillo, Angela. *Beyond the Beginnings: Literacy Interventions for Upper Elementary English Language Learners.* Clevedon, UK: Multilingual Matters, 2004.

Carter, James B. *Building Literacy Connections with Graphic Novels: Page by Page, Panel by Panel*, James B. Carter. Urbana, IL: National Council of Teachers of English, 2007.

Carter, Myron, and Christie L. Ebert. "Arts Education and 21st Century Skills." http://community.learnnc.org/dpi/music/AECoordinators.Sept08.CLErevisions.ppt.

Chabris, Christopher F. "How to Wake up Slumbering Minds." http://online.wsj.com/article/SB124079001063757515.html.

Claggett, Fran, and Joan Brown. *Drawing Your Own Conclusions: Graphic Strategies for Reading, Writing, and Thinking.* Portsmouth, NH: Heinemann, 1992.

Claggett, Fran, Louann Reid, and Ruth Vinz. *Daybook of Critical Reading and Writing: World Literature.* Wilmington, DE: Great Source Education Group, 2008.

Claggett, Fran, Louann Reid, and Ruth Vinz. *Daybook of Critical Reading and Writing.* Wilmington, MA: Great Source Education Group, 1998.

Clinton, Catherine, ed. *A Poem of Her Own: Voices of American Women Yesterday and Today.* New York: Harry N. Abrams, 2003.

"CML's Five Key Questions and CML's Core Concepts." http://www.medialit.org/sites/default/files/14A_CCKQposter.pdf (December 18, 2018).

Coffey, Heather. "Code-Switching." UNC School of Education. http://www.learnnc.org/lp/pages/4558 (March 16, 2012).

Cooley, Mason. "Mason Cooley Quotes." Brainy Quotes. http://www.brainyquote.com/quotes/quotes/m/masoncoole396165.html (September 8, 2009).

Daniels, Harvey, and Steven Zememan. "Conferences: The Core of the Workshop." In *Teaching the Best Practice Way: Methods that Matter, K–12*, Harvey Daniels and Marilyn Bazaar. Portland, ME: Stenhouse Press, 2005. www.stenhouse.com.

Dickens, Charles. *A Christmas Carol.* New York: Viking, 2000.

"Education: The What, Why, and How of 21st Century Teaching & Learning." http://www.pearltrees.com/#/N-p=34752422&N-play=1&N-u=1_494424&N-fa=4099999&N-s=1_4100175&N-f=1_4100175 (December 18, 2018).

Ellison, Ralph. "Hidden Name: Complex Fate." In *Shadow and Act*, Ralph W. Ellison. New York: Random House, 1964.

"English Language Arts Standards Anchor Standards College and Career Readiness Anchor Standards for Language." *Common Core State Standards Initiative*. 2011. http://www.corestandards.org/the-standards/english-language-arts-standards/anchor-standards-6-12/college-and-career-readiness-anchor-standards-for-language/ (March 15, 2012).

Epstein, Joseph. "The Personal Essay: A Form of Discovery." In *The Norton Book of Personal Essays*, Joseph Epstein. New York: W.W. Norton, 1997.

Estrada, Ignacio. Think Exist. http://thinkexist.com/quotes/ignacio_estrada/ (March 15, 2012).

"FETC—Digital Language Arts: A 21st Century Approach to Instruction." *FETC—Digital Language Arts: A 21st Century Approach to Instruction* (September 7, 2009).

"found poem." http://www.sdcoe.k12.ca.us/score/actbank/sfound.htm (September 7, 2009).

The Free Dictionary. "Code Switch." http://encyclopedia.thefreedictionary.com/Code%20switch (March 16, 2012).

Genevieve, Nancy. *Daughter of Chaos*. Eureka, IL: Nox Press, 2002.

Gossard, Jenee. "Using Read around Groups to Establish Criteria for Good Writing." In *Practical Ideas for Teaching Writing as a Process*, Carol B. Olson. Sacramento: California Department of Education, 1987.

Gregory, Gayle H., and Lin Kuzmich. *Differentiated Literacy Strategies: For Student Growth and Achievement in Grades 7–12*. Thousand Oaks, CA: Corwin Press, 2005.

Gutièrrez, Kris. "Teaching and Learning in the 21st Century." *English Education* 32, no. 4 (2000): 290–298. http://centerk.gseis.ucla.edu/teaching_in_the_21st_century.pdf (March 16, 2012).

Hammerstein, Oscar. "Getting to Know You." Sound Track Lyrics. http://www.stlyrics.com/lyrics/thekingandi/gettingtoknowyou.htm (March 16, 2012).

Hansen, Heather. "Speak English Clearly and Grammatically, and Boost your Success!" Articles Base. http://www.articlesbase.com/communication-articles/speak-english-clearly-and-grammatically-and-boost-your-success-195745.html (March 16, 2012).

Hazell, Ed. "21st Century Teaching." *Access Learning* (2005): 8–9.

Hendrix, Sybylla Y. "Why Our Students Study Literature." Gustavus Adolphus College. http://gustavus.edu/academics/english/whystudyliterature.php.

Houghton Mifflin College Dictionary. Boston: Houghton Mifflin, 1996.

Jackson, Anthony, Gayle A. Davis, Maud Abeel, and Anne A. Bordonero. *Turning Points 2000: Educating Adolescents in the 21st Century*. New York: Teacher College Press, 2000.

Jaffe, Clella. *Public Speaking: Concepts and Skills for a Diverse Society*. 5th ed. Boston: Wadsworth, 2007.

Jago, Carol. *With Rigor for All: Teaching the Classics to Contemporary Students*. New York: Calendar Islands Publishers, 2000.

Jefferson County Schools. *Academic Vocabulary Project*. http://jc-schools.net/tutorials/vocab/TN.html (March 16, 2012).

Jolls, Tessa, and Elizabeth Thoman. *Literacy for the 21st Century: An Overview & Orientation Guide to Media Literacy Education*. 2nd ed. Center for Media Literacy, 2008. https://www.medialit.org/sites/default/files/01_MLKorientation.pdf (Accessed 31 January 2019).

Jones, David K. *Online Teen Dangers: The Five Greatest Internet Dangers Teenagers Face and What You Can Do to Protect Them*. Scotts, Valley, CA: Create Space, 2008.

Keene, Edmond O. "The Essence of Understanding." In *Adolescent Literacy: Turning Promise into Practice*, Kylene Beers and Robert Probst. Portsmouth, NH: Heinemann, 2007.

Koriyama, Naoshi. "Unfolding Bud." In *Inner Chimes: Poems on Poetry*, Bobbye S. Goldstein and J. B. Zalben. Honesdale, PA: Boyds Mills Press, 1992.

The Learning Record. "Royce Sadler: Conversations about the Learning Record." http://www.learningrecord.org/sadler.html (March 16, 2012).

León, Vicki. *Outrageous Women of the Renaissance*. New York: John Wiley, 1999.

Literature for All Students: A Sourcebook for Teachers. Sacramento: California State Department of Education, 1985.

Manguel, Alberto. *A History of Reading*. New York: Viking, 1996.

Mission, Ray, and Wendy Morgan. *Critical Literacy and the Aesthetic: Transforming the English Classroom*. Urbana, IL: National Council of Teachers of English, 2006.

Moberg, Goran. *Critical Literacy and the Aesthetic: Transforming the English Classroom*. New York: The Writing Consultant, 1984.

Mulligan, Arlene. "Opening Doors: Drama with Second Language Learners." In *Promising Practices: Unbearably Good, Teacher Tested Ideas*, Linda Scott. San Diego: Greater San Diego Council of Teachers of English, 1996.

Noden, Harry R. *Image Grammar: Using Grammatical Structures to Teach Writing*. Portsmouth, NH: Heinemann, 1999.

Northwest Regional Educational Laboratory. "Six Traits Rubric Writing Scoring Continuum." http://www.thetraits.org/pdfRubrics/6plus1traits.PDF (March 16, 2012).

"Outrageous Women of the Renaissance." http://www.education-world.com/a_books/books126.shtml (March 16, 2012).

Partnership for 21st Century Skills. "21st Century Skills Map: English." http://www.p21.org/storage/documents/21st_century_skills_english_map.pdf (March 16, 2012).

Peacock, Molly, Elise Paschen, and Neil Neches. *Poetry in Motion: 100 Poems from Subways and Buses*. New York: W.W. Norton, 1996.

Peck, Robert N. *A Day No Pigs Would Die*. New York: Alfred A. Knopf, 1972.

Plato. *The Republic*, II, III, and X. http://classics.mit.edu/Plato/republic.html (March 16, 2012).

Professional Development for 21st Century Education. "English Language Arts (Ages 11 to 15) Literacy to Learn Standards for Students and Teachers." http://www.usdlc-l2l.org/ela_mid.pdf (March 16, 2012).

Reutzel, D. Ray, and Robert B. Cooter. *Strategies for Reading Assessment and Instruction: Helping Every Child Succeed.* Upper Saddle River, NJ: Pearson/Merrill Prentice Hall, 2006.

Richardson, W. *Blogs, Wikis, Podcasts, and Other Powerful Web Tools for Classrooms.* Thousand Oaks, CA: Corwin Press, 2009.

Rostand, Edmond. *Cyrano de Bergerac.* Lowell Blair. tr. In *World Literature*, Lake Forest, IL: Glencoe MacMillan/McGraw Hill, 1992.

RubiStar. "Create Websites for Your Project Based Learning Activities." http://rubistar.4teachers.org/index.php (March 16, 2012).

Sandel, L. "Literature for the 21st Century: A Balanced Approach." *Childhood Education*, winter (1998).

Scales, Pat. "Winning Back Your Reluctant Readers." http://www.randomhouse.com/highschool/RHI_magazine/pdf/scales.pdf (March 16, 2012).

Shafer, Gregory. "Standard English and the Migrant Community." *English Journal* 90, no. 4 (2001): 37–43. http://www.ncte.org/library/NCTEFiles/Resources/Journals/EJ/0904-march01/EJ0904Standard.pdf (March 16, 2012).

Smith, David I., and Barbara M. Carvill. *The Gift of the Stranger: Faith, Hospitality, and Foreign Language Learning.* Grand Rapids, MI: William B. Eerdmans, 2000.

Standards for English Language Arts. Urbana, IL: National Council of Teachers of English, 1996.

Starr, Linda S. "Outrageous Women of the Renaissance: Warriors, Artists, Rulers, and Thieves." Education World. http://www.education-world.com/a_books/books126.shtml (March 16, 2012).

Stevenson, Chris. "Curriculum That Is Challenging, Integrative, and Exploratory." In *This We Believe—And Now We Must Act*, Thomas O. Erb. Westerville, OH: National Middle School Association, 2001.

Stone, Linda. "Continuous Partial Attention." Linda Stone. http://www.lindastone.net (March 16, 2012).

The Story of English. DVD. 2001. USA: Home Video.

Tapscott, Don. *Growing Up Digital: The Rise of the Net Generation.* New York: McGraw Hill, 1998.

Technology in the Middle. "21st Century Literacy: Basic Literacy." http://pwoessner.com/2008/11/29/21st-century-literacy-basic-literacy/ (March 16, 2012).

"Top 15 Educational Tools/Sites for Middle School Language Arts." http://theitclassroom.blogspot.com/2008/01/top-15-educational-toolssites-for.html (March 16, 2012).

Troupe, Quincy. "My Poems Have Holes Sewn Into Them." In *Transcircularities: New and Selected Poems*, Quincy Troupe, 98–99, 1st edition. Minneapolis: Coffee House Press, 2002.

Tuckman, Bruce W. "Developmental Sequence in Small Groups." University of Florida. http://aneesha.ceit.uq.edu.au/drupal/sites/default/files/Tuckman%201965.pdf (March 16, 2012).

"21st Century Skills." http://www.thinkfinity.org/21st-century-skills (March 16, 2012).

Vincent, Tony. "Learning in Hand." http://learninginhand.com/blog/ (March 16, 2012).

Ward, William Arthur. "Quotes about Teaching." National Education Association. 2012. http://www.nea.org/grants/17417.htm (March 8, 2012).

Wiesel, Elie. *Night*. New York: Bantam, 1982.

Williams, Raymond. *Keywords: A Vocabulary of Culture and Society*. New York: Oxford University Press, 1976.

Williams, Terry, and Jenny Williams. Image, Word, Poem: Visual Literacy and the Writing Process (workshop for National Council of Teachers of English at Detroit Institute of Art). 1997.

Wolterstorff, Nicholas. *Works and Worlds of Art*. New York: Oxford University Press, 1980.

Word Net Search. Princeton, NJ: Princeton University, http://wordnetweb.princeton.edu/perl/webwn?s=renaissance (March 16, 2012).

Wordle. http://www.wordle.net/ (March 16, 2012).

Zenkel, Suzanne S, ed. *For My Teacher*. White Plains, NY: Peter Pauper, 1994.

Zimmermann, Susan, and Chryse Hutchins. *Seven Keys to Comprehension: How to Help Your Kids Read It and Get It*. New York: Three Rivers Press, 2003.

About the Author

Anna J. Small Roseboro, a National Board Certified Teacher, has over four decades experience teaching in public and private schools, mentoring early career educators, and facilitating leadership institutes. She was awarded Distinguished Service Awards by the California Association of Teachers of English (2009) and the National Council of Teachers of English (2016).

Roseboro earned a BA in speech communications from Wayne State University and an MA in curriculum design from the University of California, San Diego. Her research investigated the link between writing to learn and retention in mathematics. She earned the Early Adolescent/ English Language Arts Certificate from the National Board of Professional Teaching Standards in 1998.

Mrs. Roseboro represented Rotary International in a group-study exchange with educators in East Africa. In addition to teaching young adolescents in Michigan, Missouri, New York, Massachusetts, and California, she has taught adults at the Rochester Theological Institute, Grand Valley State University, and Calvin College. She served sixteen years as director of summer session programs for students in grades five through twelve, coached a National Forensic League competitive speech team for twelve years, and was English Department chair from 1999 to 2005 at the Bishop's School. In 2008/2009, Anna was a faculty leader at the NCTE Affiliate and Leadership Conference and served as master teacher for the San Francisco Bay Area Teachers Center in an online teaching environment.

Her articles have appeared in the *English Journal*, *English Leadership Quarterly*, *Fine Lines*—a national quarterly creative writing journal, and *California English*. She has published three texts for teachers: Teaching

Middle School Language Arts (2010), *Teaching Writing in the Middle School* (2013), and *Teaching Reading in the Middle School* (2013); a novel and a poetry book for young people. Her writing appears in online professional blogs, in online communities for teachers such as English Companion and the Teaching and Learning Forum, and in *Continuing the Journey: Becoming a Better Teacher of Literature and Informational Texts* (2017).

Since her retirement, Mrs. Roseboro serves as codirector of the Conference on English Education Commission to Support Early Career English Language Arts Teachers and of the National Council of Teachers of English Early Career Educators of Color Leadership Award Program.

www.ingramcontent.com/pod-product-compliance
Lightning Source LLC
Chambersburg PA
CBHW021850300426
44115CB000C5B/92